THE GARDEN LIBRARY

ANNUALS
AND
BIENNIALS

THE GARDEN LIBRARY

ANNUALS
AND
BIENNIALS

Kenneth A. Beckett

BALLANTINE BOOKS · NEW YORK

Editor
Anthony Livesey

Designer
Julia Harris

Managing Editor
Jackie Douglas

Art Director
Roger Bristow

Consultants
Margaret McQuade Hagedorn
James Fanning

First published in Great Britain in 1984 by
Dorling Kindersley Limited

The Garden Library ANNUALS and BIENNIALS was conceived,
edited and designed by Dorling Kindersley Limited,
9 Henrietta Street, London WC2E 8PS

Library of Congress Catalog Card Number: 83-91181

ISBN 0-345-30908-1

Manufactured in the United States of America

First Ballantine Books Trade Edition: April 1984
10 9 8 7 6 5 4 3 2 1

Contents

A border devoted to annuals can be made one of the most colorful features of a garden. Plant the taller, bolder specimens at the back, with progressively shorter species and cultivars in front of them.

Care and cultivation

Annuals are the gardener's standby, providing color in the shortest possible time for a minimum of expenditure. They are also ideal plants to decorate a newly cleared garden while plans are made for permanent subjects. Annuals are so called because their entire lives are encompassed in a single growing season. From seed sown in spring, plants start to flower from early to mid-summer and die in the fall. These, the true annuals, include such favorites as *Amaranthus caudatus* (love-lies-bleeding), *Tagetes erecta* and *Tagetes patula* (African and French marigolds), *Iberis umbellata* (candytuft) and *Nigella damascena* (love-in-a-mist). In addition, there are several perennial plants that flower the first season and are usually classified among the annuals. Familiar examples are *Antirrhinum majus* (snapdragon) and *Ricinus communis* (castor-oil-plant or bean). Whether true annuals or merely classified as such, these plants can be divided into two broad groups: those that need to be raised in the warmth of a greenhouse or on a sunny window-ledge and those that can be sown where they are to grow.

Biennials are equally showy, but their life cycle extends over most of two growing seasons. Sown in late spring or early summer, they form leafy plants, often of rosetted form, which become mature by the fall. The following spring they resume growth and thrust up flower stems, which bloom during the summer and then die. Their main disadvantage is that a plot of land must be set aside for their first season's growth or, if they are sited in the main garden, one must be prepared for foliage alone the first year. However, where they can be fitted in they make a very rewarding display. Annuals, and to a lesser extent biennials, are adaptable plants and can have a variety of roles in the garden.

Annual beds and borders

To get the maximum floral impact from annuals, whole beds and borders should be devoted to them alone. Tastefully planned, they can provide a display unequalled by any other plant group. Small beds should contain one or two different sorts, larger ones a greater variety. For the best effect, sow or plant each species, variety or cultivar in a group or drift of not less than ten plants. Fewer than this will create a spotty or jumbled effect.

People see and react to colors in different ways. Some people enjoy the clash of bright colors, others prefer a more muted effect. When planning an annual border there is much to be said for following the recommendations of that famous Victorian and Edwardian gardener, Gertrude Jekyll. Basically, one end of the bed or border is planted with pastel shades, then with progressively stronger colors that reach a climax of brilliance. If the border is long enough, this climax could be in the middle, fading to paler colors at each end. Not only should the display be graded by shades of color but also by the actual colors. Color clash can be avoided by following the sequence yellow, orange, red, violet, blue, green.

The shape, texture and color of foliage should not be ignored. Although annuals are esteemed mainly for their flowers, there are several kinds noteworthy for their ornamental leaves. These can be used to combine or contrast with the flowers and will add distinction to a massed display of blossom. Good examples of foliage annuals are *Amaranthus caudatus* 'Joseph's-coat', *Ricinus communis* (castor-oil-plant) and *Kochia scoparia* (summer cypress).

Mixed borders

Both annuals and biennials can be used effectively in mixed borders of trees, shrubs, hardy perennials and bulbs. Leave spaces among the permanent plants, ideally with some attractive foliage shrubs as a background; something different can be grown every year. Alternatively, areas of spring bulbs and perennials can be interplanted with annuals, which will take over when their host's flowering season has passed.

Containers

Bulbs, annuals and perennials are the most useful of all plants for containers, such as window-boxes, tubs and hanging baskets. Two or even three displays a year can be planned and, if thought is given to the choice of species and cultivars, the changes can be rung almost indefinitely. An enormous amount of satisfaction can be gained from the

Almost any container can be planted with annuals, from simple pots to elaborate patio tubs (far left) and window-boxes (center). A strawberry pot or barrel (below), well planted, makes an attractive feature on a terrace.

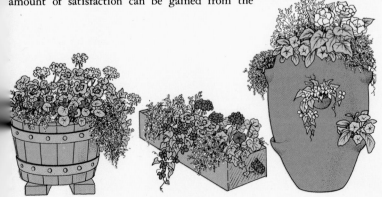

planning and planting of a window-box or urn. There is a temptation to crowd in the greatest variety of plants possible and, if well organized, this can look charming. Generally, however, the best effects are the simplest, such as one sort of foliage plant surrounded by, or set beside, one or two sorts of flowering plant. *Kochia scoparia* (summer cypress), for example, makes a good foliage centerpiece for an urn or tub and looks attractive surrounded by something low growing, such as *Nemophila Menziesii*, *Phacelia campanularia* (Californian bluebell) or a dwarf *Antirrhinum*, for example 'Tom Thumb'.

Pot plants

Some of the best known pot plants for the greenhouse or home are annuals or biennials. In addition to the largely tender, time-honored greenhouse pot plants, many of the hardy annuals make very successful pot plants for the cold or barely heated greenhouse. Particularly effective when grown in this way are *Antirrhinum majus* (snapdragon), *Campanula medium* (Canterbury bells), *Clarkia pulchella*, *Kochia scoparia* (summer cypress), *Viola* × *Wittrockiana* (pansy), *Phlox Drummondii* and *Matthiola incana* (stock). Practically all the hardy and half-hardy annuals and biennials are worth trying as pot specimens. Most of the hardy sorts do not need sowing until the fall and the tender ones can be left until late winter or early spring.

Cutting

Annuals and biennials are indispensable to those flower arrangers who like to grow their own floral material. Rather than robbing the main garden display, it is worthwhile setting aside a strip of ground, perhaps at the edge of the vegetable plot, where favorite annuals can be sown in rows for the sole purpose of cutting.

Screening

Climbing annuals can be used very effectively to cover unsightly objects or areas and as a summer screen, either around a sitting-out area or between ornamental and vegetable plots. *Lathyrus odoratus* (sweet peas) and *Tropaeolum peregrinum* (canary-bird vine) are perfect choices, but there are several others well worth giving a trial, notably *Ipomoea purpurea* (morning-glory) and *Thunbergia alata* (black-eyed Susan vine).

Soil

All the popular and most of the less well known annuals and biennials are tolerant of a wide range of

Some annuals, such as these Impatiens, *make splendid pot plants for a cold greenhouse, or grouped in a variety of ways on a patio to provide color.*

Climbing annuals, such as Lathyrus odoratus *(sweet pea) and* Ipomoea purpurea *(morning-glory), make excellent temporary screens to mask trash cans, for example, from a patio or terrace in summer.*

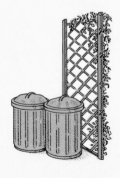

soil conditions. For the best results, however, the soil must be well drained and fertile. A fertile soil is one well laced with organic matter, which contains the essential substance called humus. The name humus is often used for the organic matter itself, for example farmyard or stable manure, garden compost, peat and so on, but it is actually a complex colloidal substance which coats the soil particles and holds water and dissolved mineral salts. Sandy and chalky soils and the stickier sorts of clay need plenty of organic matter. Ideally, at least one, and preferably two, gallon bucketsful should be applied to each square yard. This is best done in the fall or winter, but can be carried out at any time prior to sowing or planting. Whatever the nature of the organic matter, it should be spread evenly and forked into the top spit (one spade's depth). Just before sowing or planting out, apply a dressing of general fertilizer according to makers' instructions and rake into the surface. A slow release, granular fertilizer is best.

The soil for containers such as pots, urns, tubs and window-boxes needs to be somewhat richer than that in the garden because the root system of a plant in a container is confined to a much smaller volume of soil than it would normally occupy in an outside bed. For the best results, use a commercial potting mix. All of those available in shops are satisfactory, though in general those that are soil-based have the edge over the all-peat types. Ordinary garden soil can be used but it needs to be mixed with an equal volume of organic matter. Peat moss, also called moss peat, is the easiest and cleanest substance to use but it must be accompanied by a good general fertilizer, preferably of the slow-release sort. To each bushel (a box 22 × 10 × 10 in, 55 × 25 × 25 cm) of soil and peat mix, in proportions suitable for the plants in question, add 6–8 oz (165–225 gm) of fertilizer to supply the necessary mineral foods that plants

Many garden plants, both annuals and biennials, thrive best in humus-rich soils. To provide a regular supply of organic matter, install a three-component compost bin, filling each in turn with leaves, non-seeding annual weeds, grass mowings and vegetable trimmings from the kitchen.

require. If acid soil is used, then 3–6 oz of lime should be added. However good the basic mix, vigorous plants will soon use up the main minerals and supplementary feeding will be necessary. This is most easily achieved by applying a liquid fertilizer, made up and used according to makers' instructions. Liquid feeding should start about six weeks after planting or final potting.

Situation

All the most popular annuals and biennials need a sunny site if sturdy, free-flowering plants are to develop. The minimum requirement of sunshine is half a day, unobstructed by trees or buildings. There are some exceptions, however, that will give a reasonable performance with only a few hours sun each day: *Antirrhinum majus* (snapdragon), *Campanula medium* (Canterbury bells), *Cheiranthus Cheiri* (wallflower), *Digitalis purpurea* (foxglove), *Iberis umbellata* (candytuft), *Lunaria annua* (honesty) and *Viola* × *Wittrockiana* (pansy).

Most of the taller annuals, those above 2–3 ft (60–90 cm) in height, are best in a situation sheltered from the strongest winds. However, annuals are on the whole fairly wind-proof, especially if grown *en masse* with each plant protecting its neighbor. If necessary, give plants extra support (see 'Supporting plants', page 11).

Planting

Tender annuals and those hardy ones traditionally raised in warmth in late winter or early spring, such as *Antirrhinum*, are planted out when fear of further frost has passed. Tip the plants out of their containers or cut out individually with the point of a sharp trowel or kitchen knife. The separated plants must then be laid out in their correct positions and planted with a trowel. Dig a hole a little larger than the root ball, set the young plant in position a fraction lower than it was in the container and then fill in the gaps and firm down with the fingers. If the weather is warm and dry, the plants should be well watered to settle them in.

The easiest way to remove young plants from the flat or seed-box in which they have been grown is to take off one side and slide them out. If, however, you wish to re-use the flat, first thump each end firmly on the ground (below) to loosen the plants, then lift them out. Separate the plants (below right) and set them in their permanent sites at once (below, far right).

The distance apart at which to set a batch of young plants often presents a problem to the beginner, and annuals and biennials are no exception. Much depends on the ultimate height and spread of each plant. As a rule-of-thumb, a suitable distance apart is that equal to half the ultimate height of the species or cultivar concerned. Tall, thin species can be set a little closer together. Where two species adjoin in beds and borders, the distance between them can be arrived at by combining their total heights and dividing by four.

Feeding

Providing the soil is fertile from previous cultivation or prepared in the way outlined above, annuals and biennials in the open ground should not need any supplementary feeding. For various reasons, however, it may be necessary to carry out sowing or planting without preparation. As a result, the seedlings of young plants may grow very slowly or look starved. In such a situation, a light dressing of a high nitrogen fertilizer is advisable. If a comparatively small number of plants are concerned, there is much to be said for applying the high nitrogen fertilizer in liquid form. Nitrogen must not be over-applied as too much can result in exuberant leafy growth at the expense of flowers. Two weeks after the nitrogen feed, apply a general, slow-release fertilizer.

Unless the soil is known to be rich in plant foods, a dressing of fertilizer before sowing or setting out the young plants is advisable. Avoid a high nitrogen feed, unless the young plants are yellowish and wilting.

Supporting plants

There are many dwarf, wind-proof annuals that do not need supporting, but to use these exclusively can create a rather uninspiring, flat or uniform effect. Taller species and cultivars are needed to give the height and depth that lends character to a display. Regrettably, many otherwise decorative annuals are prone to wind and rain damage once they exceed about 2 ft (60 cm) in height. The easiest way to overcome this problem is to surround each group of taller annuals with twiggy pea sticks, often called pea brush. Choose sticks that, when pushed firmly into the soil, stand no more than half the ultimate height of the plants. Once the plants are grown and start to flower, the sticks will be fully masked from view. The best time to put in supporting sticks is when the seedlings are a few inches tall or after young plants are set out.

Maintenance

Once the seedlings are growing or the young plants set out, the primary maintenance chore is weeding. This should be attended to regularly, particularly during the seedling stage for competition from fast growing weeds can slow down or stifle seedling annuals. Once the plants touch each other, it is the weed seedlings that cannot take a hold and from then on the weeding chore ceases.

Watering should be carried out during spells of drought, especially while the plants are small. When the plants are in full bloom, dead-heading is worthwhile though not essential. Removing spent flower heads, and thus preventing the plant from putting its energies into seed production, tends to prolong the floral display but not as dramatically as some gardening authorities suggest.

Propagation

True annuals and biennials can only be increased by seeds. However, as stated earlier, some plants grown as annuals are, in reality, short lived perennials and these can be propagated by cuttings or division.

Seed sowing

To prepare a flat for sowing, fill with soil just proud of the rim, then rap gently on a hard surface to settle it. Scrape off the surplus soil level with the rim and firm with a presser.

If more than one type of seed is to be sown in the same flat, make a series of small drills about 1½ in (4 cm) apart and ¼ in (6 mm) deep, using the edge of a ruler or a strip of board.

SEED Annuals and biennials can be raised in the warmth of the home or a greenhouse and the plants set outside later, or they can be sown where they are to grow. In general, the sorts tender to frost should be raised under cover, the hardy ones sown outside. In the cooler climates, the tender sorts are known as half-hardy and are sown in a warm place as a matter of course. In warmer climates that do not experience spring frosts, they can be sown where they are ultimately to grow.

Seed may either be bought or, since all the true annuals and biennials produce plenty of seeds if they are not regularly dead-headed, taken from your own plants. Collect seeds only from the best plants and ensure that they are mature. This means waiting until the seed heads or pods turn yellow or brown and start to split or fall. They must then be gathered and kept dry and moderately warm. Seed pods that split explosively, as do those of lupins, for example, must be kept in paper bags. Once the seeds are thoroughly dry, they must be placed in packets, with a record of their name and date of harvesting attached. Store them in a cool, dry place until sowing time.

Nowadays, an increasing number of annuals are the result of scientific plant breeding, the best example being the so-called F1 Hybrids. These do not come true to type from home-saved seed and must be purchased from a reputable seedsman.

SOWING UNDER GLASS If half-hardy annuals are sown in the greenhouse or home, shallow containers and a weed-free, seed-sowing mix must be used. The size of the container depends on the number of plants required. If 10–20 plants of each annual are sufficient, 2½–3 in (6–7.5 cm) pots are big enough. Larger numbers will need 5–6 in (13–15 cm) pans or a bigger seed tray (box or flat). It is best to use a commercial seed-sowing mix to be sure there are no weed seeds or pests and diseases present that might harm the seedlings. Fill the containers with the mixture, then press it down firmly but gently so that a gap ½–¾ in (1–2 cm) deep is left between the soil surface and the rim of the receptacle. Drainage material is not needed in the small or shallow containers used for seed sowing. The seeds must be sown thinly, as over-crowded seedlings are prone to damping-off disease. Very fine seeds, such as begonia and antirrhinum, are best mixed with several volumes (at least five) of fine dry sand. The mixture should then be sown as if the whole lot were seed. If they are large enough to handle with the fingers or tweezers, there is much to be said for space sowing – that is, setting the seeds ½–1½ in (1–4 cm) apart, depending on size. For example, *Iberis umbellata* (candytuft) can be given the smallest spacing, *Lathyrus odoratus* (sweet peas) and *Tropaeolum majus* (nasturtiums) the largest. The very fine seeds do not need covering with seed-sowing mix, but all others should be covered with a depth equal to the diameter of the seed concerned.

Sow the seed evenly and thinly. If the seeds are too small to handle easily, mix them with several volumes of fine, dry sand and sow the mixture as if it were all seed. Make a note of what has been sown.

When sowing is completed, the seed-sowing mix must be thoroughly moistened, either with a fine-rosed can or by immersing the containers in water up to, or just below, the soil level. This immersion method is best for fine seeds. Once the surface of the seed-sowing mix is wet, the containers must be removed from the water, allowed to drain and then placed in a propagating case (a glass- or clear-plastic-covered structure, often incorporating removable lights), or on a greenhouse bench or a window-ledge indoors.

As soon as the seed is sown, cover with soil and water thoroughly. Use a fine-rosed watering can or set the flat in a tray of water until air bubbles cease erupting.

Apart from those put in a propagating case, the sown containers should be covered with a sheet of glass or plastic to prevent rapid drying out of the potting mix during the critical germination period. A warm temperature is needed, about 60°F (16°C), though germination will be faster and sometimes more profuse at 65–70°F (18–20°C). Most hardy annuals will germinate at lower temperatures, from 55–60°F (13–16°C). Temperatures above those recommended can be damaging and inhibit germination. For this reason, the glass- or plastic-covered seed containers must not be left in direct sunlight. Either put them in a shady place or cover with sheets of newspaper.

After three to five days, look at the containers daily for signs of germination and remove excess condensation from the covers. As soon as the seedlings are seen crooking through the soil, remove the cover and place the container in good light. For the next few days they must be screened from direct sunlight; thereafter, only shading from the hottest sunlight is necessary. It is important to foster sturdy, short-jointed young plants, so they should be given as much light as they will take. If the seedlings bend sharply toward the source of light, they need more. Moving them nearer to the source will help and, in the home, turning the container around each day will keep them straight. If natural daylight is poor, as it can be in late winter and early spring, the seedlings can be placed under a fluorescent strip light that does not give off too much heat. Manufacturers give guidance on positioning the light above the potting mix.

As soon as the seedlings' leaves are fully expanded and the true or rough leaves begin to show, it is time to space them out in larger containers. This is known as pricking off. Seedlings in pots and pans can be knocked out in a block by inverting the container and rapping the edge on a wooden surface, but seedlings in boxes must be carefully dug out in small clumps with a widger or old kitchen knife. Fill larger containers with potting compost and space out the seedlings 1½–2 in (4–5 cm) apart each way.

Use a widger or dibber to make the holes. A dibber is a blunt-ended stick, varying in thickness according to the size of the seedlings being dealt with. The very tiny seedlings of begonia and lobelia can be extremely fiddly to prick off, as they need attending to when they are almost too small to handle. Some gardeners and nurserymen take the easy way out, pricking off these tiny seedlings in small clumps. To deal with them properly, use the following technique.

Cut a notch into the end of a small wooden or plastic label. Then loosen the seedlings with the pointed end. Next, turn the label around so that it can be used like a fork. By gently pushing the notch just beneath the pair of seed leaves, it is easy to transfer a seedling to its dibber hole and firm it in position. Water the seedlings and return to the same growing conditions as before.

Annuals being raised for an open garden display must be left to grow-on in these larger containers until they are ready for final planting but those destined to be used for a cold or cool greenhouse display will need potting singly. As a rough guide, it is time to pot once the leaves of the young plant start to touch or just overlap at the tips. An average container size for first potting is 3 in (7.5 cm).

CUTTINGS Several plants grown as annuals are in reality perennials and include some species of *Centaurea* and *Dahlia*, *Dianthus barbatus* (sweet William) and *D. chinensis* (rainbow pink), *Heliotropium arborescens* (heliotrope), *Mirabilis jalapa* (Marvel-of-Peru), and *Verbena* hybrids. All are frost tender and in areas with cold winters must be dug up and kept in a frost-free place or cool greenhouse. Cut back the plants by about a half, pot them and keep just moist. In the late winter to spring period, young shoots will form and, when well grown, can be taken as cuttings.

An alternative is to take cuttings from the plants while they are still growing at the end of summer or very early fall. Such cuttings are short lengths of young stem with leaves. They are known as softwood cuttings to distinguish them from the woody ones used to propagate shrubs and trees. Softwood cuttings are usually stem tips or whole shoots, 2–4 in (5–10 cm) in length. Each must be severed cleanly with a sharp knife or razor blade just below a node (leaf joint). Nip or sever the leaves from the lower half of the stem, dip the base of the stem in a hormone rooting powder combined with a fungicide and then insert the cuttings in a suitable rooting medium. An ideal rooting medium is one made up of equal amounts of peat moss passed through a ¼ in (6 mm) sieve, and coarse, washed sand, fine grit or perlite. Enclose the cuttings in a propagating case or plastic bag to maintain humidity. Bottom heat to maintain a temperature of 60–65°F (16–18°C) will speed rooting. When well rooted and starting to grow from the tips, plant each cutting singly in a container of potting mix. Subsequent treatment is as for seedlings.

HARDENING-OFF Plants intended for the garden must be acclimatized to open air and direct sunlight before planting out, a procedure known as hardening-off. The sequence is as follows. First, lower the temperature of the greenhouse or room (if artificial heat is being used) and give more ventilation. After about seven to ten days, preferably move the plants to a cold frame, which should be well ventilated by day but closed at night. If there is no frame, stand the plant container outside in a sheltered, sunny spot during the day but take it inside again during the early evening or before nightfall. After a further seven to ten days, take off the frame tops or leave plants outside in the sheltered spot all the time. The whole hardening-off process should take not less than two and preferably three weeks, but much depends on the weather at the time. Hardening-off must be

Taking cuttings

Take cuttings from healthy, non-flowering growth, ideally basal shoots or those low down on strong stems.

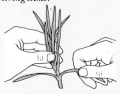

Carefully remove the lower leaves by pulling or pinching them with the nails of thumb and index finger.

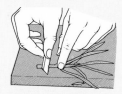

Sever the stem cleanly beneath a node, using a sharp knife or razor blade. This is best done by cutting down on a wood surface.

Insert the completed cuttings around the edges of quick draining soil and place in a propagating case.

timed to coincide with the expected last spring frost
so that when planted in their permanent site they will
not suffer damaging shock to their growth.

SOWING ON SITE Most hardy annuals and biennials
are best sown where they are intended to flower.
The soil, ideally prepared previously as described
above, must be free of weeds. If recently dug, it
should be lightly tamped to firm the surface, then
raked level. Seed can either be sown in drills (narrow
row furrows made in the soil) or broadcast. To
make drills, place a straight-edged board or garden
line in position and use a pointed stick or the corner
of a hoe blade. The drills must be shallow, ¼ in
(6 mm) being deep enough for the majority of
annuals and biennials. Larger seeds, such as
Lunaria annua (honesty), *Lathyrus odoratus* (sweet
pea) and *Tropaeolum majus* (nasturtium), need
deeper drills to allow a soil covering equal to the
diameter of a seed. After sowing, fill the drills in
and lightly firm with the back of a rake.

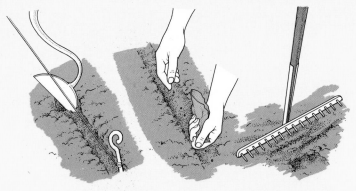

*When sowing on site, make
sure the soil has been
enriched with organic
matter or fertilizer, then
lightly firm with the feet
and rake to a fine tilth.
Using a line or board,
draw out the shallow drills
with a hoe (above) and sow
the seed thinly (above,
right). Cover and firm with
a rake (above, far right).*

Where annuals are used in blocks or drifts, as in
an annual or mixed border, broadcast sowing is
often the easier method. Mark out the site to be
sown with a pointed stick and scatter the seed
thinly. Firmly but gently rake in one direction
across the sown area, and then again at right angles
to the first raking, to cover the seed. If dry weather
persists after sowing, water with a fine-rosed can.
When the seedlings have grown to the point where
their first true (rough) leaves are showing, thin
their permanent spacing.

Pests and diseases

Healthy plants, that is those in fertile soil with
adequate moisture and sunshine, tend to suffer few
pest and disease problems. When infestations
occur, they must be dealt with promptly before
lasting damage is done. If it is necessary to use

chemical sprays, they must be applied strictly to makers' instructions. If too strong, they may damage the plant; if too weak, they will not be effective in dealing with either fungus or insects.

Mildly to badly malformed leaves and stems are usually the result of the feeding habits of piercing and sucking insects. Most commonly seen are the various sorts of aphid or plant lice, also known as greenfly and blackfly. They are tiny, soft, oval-bodied, sometimes winged insects which cluster thickly on the undersides of leaves or on stem tips. They are easily killed with a contact or systemic insecticide. Small attacks can be dealt with by wetting with warm, soapy water.

If the deformation of leaves is accompanied by a rather tattered appearance, often with holes of a regular size, then capsids or plant bugs are the cause. These are like large aphids, but are fast moving and secretive. The observable damage is the result of much earlier feeding, piercing the tender shoot tips. If attacks occur regularly, applications of insecticide must start in late spring.

Stunting and crippling of stems can also be caused by the immature (nymphal) stage of froghoppers or spittlebugs. This pest is easily recognized by the spit-like blobs of plant sap which shelters the insect. Small infestations can be squashed; larger ones need spraying.

Pieces eaten out of leaf or petal margins usually indicate that caterpillars or earwigs are feeding. Where damage is slight, it is worthwhile looking for the pest and simply removing it from the plant. Larger infestations must be sprayed. Earwigs and some caterpillars hide by day and feed only at night. Plants attacked by these are best sprayed or dusted with a commercial insecticide at ten-day intervals. Earwigs can be trapped in small pots filled with dry straw, hay or crumpled paper, secured to sticks placed among the plants.

Irregular nibbled patches, especially on young leaves at or near ground level, are probably caused by slugs or snails. Silvery slime trails will reveal this. An approved slug killer can be applied; alternatively, snails can be trapped by laying old lettuce leaves, grapefruit skins or moist bran in the area. The traps must be inspected early each morning.

Sometimes the leaves and young shoots of a single stem or whole plant are covered with, or bear patches of, a whitish or pale gray, somewhat powdery film. This is mildew. Attacked leaves yellow or wither prematurely and die, weakening the plant and making it unsightly. Control is not always easy, but spraying with a commercial fungicide is usually successful.

Aphid bugs suck the sap from the roots and upper parts of a plant, causing weakness and yellowing.

Capsid bugs feed by piercing and sucking the sap from young shoot tips. Embryo leaves become tattered and have holes.

Young spittle bugs suck plant sap and cause deformities on young leaves and shoots.

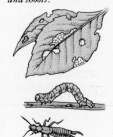

Caterpillars feed on the edges of mature leaves; earwigs attack young leaves and flowers.

Ageratum houstonianum

Ageratum

Very few of the 60 species in this genus are cultivated, but one has become a universal favorite for summer beds and borders. This is *A. houstonianum*, the flossflower from Mexico, a branched plant to 2 ft (60 cm) tall with heart-shaped leaves. It bears a profusion of flower heads like tiny pompons in shades of purple-blue, pink or white. Although an excellent plant for cutting, its many dwarf cultivars are the ones usually seen. These have a very compact habit, are 5–8 in (13–20 cm) in height and bloom well into the fall.

Propagation *Seed is the usual method. Sow in a warm temperature (about 60–65°F, 16–18°C) around mid-spring. Harden-off the seedlings in a cold frame before planting outside.*

Soil *Ordinary, well-drained garden soil is suitable. Too rich a medium will encourage lush foliage at the expense of flowers.*

Position *A site in full sun is best, but a little shade is tolerated.*

Cultivation *Young plants must not be put out until fear of frost has passed. The tall cultivars will be bushier if the leading shoots are pinched out when the young plants are 3–4 in (7.5–10 cm) tall.*

Pinch out the growing points of tall cultivars when the plants are 4–6 in (10–15 cm) in height. Bushier, more shapely plants will result, giving greater impact in a bedding scheme. Bushy plants will also provide more stems for cutting but, in this case, the soil must be fertile to ensure they reach full height.

Alcea rosea

Alcea

This genus is still frequently listed under the more familiar Latin name *Althaea* and is commonly known as hollyhock. Most widely grown is *A. rosea*, which has large maple-shaped leaves and 6–10 ft (1.8–3 m) tall spires of wide, open flowers. Several cultivars and strains are known with single or double flowers in shades of red, pink, white and yellow. Some cultivars have deeply lobed leaves and are of hybrid origin with *A. ficifolia* (the fig-leaved hollyhock). Although strictly perennials, most will flower the first year from seed and are usually grown as annuals or biennials.

Propagation *Seed is the usual method. Grown as an annual, seed must be sown in early spring at a medium temperature, about 55–60°F (13–16°C). As a biennial, sow the seeds outside in late spring or early summer.*
Soil *Ordinary garden soil, well-drained and fertile but not over rich, is the ideal. The richer the soil the taller the plants.*
Position *A sunny site is necessary, though a little shade in the morning or afternoon is tolerated.*
Cultivation *Sow seeds for annual plants in their permanent position, those for biennials in nursery rows. Move these to their permanent sites as soon as they have about three leaves.*

In double flowers, some or all stamens have become petal-like. The 'powder-puff' flower (far right) is an example where the stamens have turned into full-length petals. In the anemone-centered bloom (right) half-length petals have formed a central boss.

Amaranthus tricolor 'Joseph's-Coat'

Amaranthus

The species *A. caudatus*, love-lies-bleeding or tassel flower, is the best known member of this genus of 60 species of annuals. Its hanging clusters of thick, red, catkin-like flower spikes are intriguing and immediately recognizable. *A.c.* 'Viridis' has pale green flowers, while 'Green Balls' has its lime-green spikes broken into ball-like clusters. All are good material for the flower arranger. *A. tricolor* has insignificant flowers but highly colored foliage, which can be oval in outline or almost ribbon-like. In the cultivar 'Joseph's-Coat', the leaves are patterned bronze, red and yellow.

Propagation *Seed is the only means, and must be sown in a warm temperature (about 70°F, 21°C) from early to mid-spring. Bigger specimens will result if the young plants are moved into 4–5 in (10–13 cm) pots.*
Soil *Ordinary fertile soil is suitable, well-drained but never dry.*
Position *Although a little shade is tolerated, a site with plenty of sun is best.*
Cultivation *Young plants must not be put out until all fear of frost has passed and the weather warmed up. They should be allowed to grow naturally, as pinching reduces the size of flower spikes and leaves.*

A. caudatus, *aptly known as love-lies-bleeding or tassel flower, is native to the tropics. The young leaves are edible and are grown as a food in India. In rich soil and a warm climate the plant can achieve 5 ft (1.5 m) in height. Under ordinary soil conditions, it averages about 3 ft (90 cm) and can be even smaller if the young plants suffer root disturbance or drought.*

Anchusa capensis

Anchusa

This genus provides some splendid, blue-flowered hardy perennials, rock plants and at least one showy biennial. This last, *A. capensis* from South Africa, can also be grown as an annual. It forms a rosette of narrowly lance-shaped, dark green leaves to 6 in (15 cm) in length. From the center rise branched, leafy stems 1–1½ ft (30–45 cm) tall, each bearing several sprays of five-petalled blue, white or pink flowers with white throats and red edges. All bloom from summer through fall.

Propagation *Seed is the only method and, as an annual, should be sown in early spring in a warm temperature of about 60°F (16°C). In areas of mild winters, it can be sown in summer for blooming in the following spring.*
Soil *Ordinary well-drained garden soil is best. Too rich a medium will encourage leaf at the expense of flowers.*
Position *A sunny site is best, though a little shade is tolerated. Hot and humid conditions are not appreciated.*
Cultivation *Although fairly hardy, young plants should not be set outside until there is no further fear of frost.*

For a formal design in a bed or border of annuals, use the edge of a thin board to mark out a grid in the newly raked soil. Informal patterns can be drawn free-hand with a blunt-ended stick. Use only one type of plant in each of the segments.

Antirrhinum majus

Antirrhinum

Snapdragons are among the most popular of summer flowering annuals. All the many kinds listed by seedsmen are derived from one species, *A. majus*, a native of south-western Europe and technically a perennial. The closed-mouth, tubular flowers come in shades of pink to red-purple, yellow and white. Some of the more curious mutant strains have open-mouthed flowers, while others are double. Sizes range from only 4–6 in (10–15 cm) tall to 3 ft (90 cm) in height.

Propagation *All the modern cultivars are raised annually from seed sown in early spring at a medium temperature of 55–60°F (13–16°C). Prick off the tiny seedlings as soon as they are large enough to handle. It is possible to overwinter plants, and to take cuttings in spring.*
Soil *Well-drained but otherwise ordinary garden soil is suitable. Too rich a medium will result in soft, disease-prone growth.*
Position *A sunny site is best, though some shade is tolerated.*
Cultivation *Young plants are reasonably hardy but frost will kill them.*

During its many years in cultivation, natural mutation and the work of plant breeders have produced a wide selection of habits, heights, flower forms and colors of antirrhinum.

Dwarf cultivar

Tall cultivar

Penstemon-flowered type

Begonia semperflorens

Begonia

Of the 900 known species in this genus, one is pre-eminent as a colorful and long-flowering summer bedding plant. This is *B. semperflorens*, technically an evergreen perennial, from Brazil. Known as wax begonia from the texture of both leaves and flowers, it is a bushy plant up to about 1 ft (30 cm) in height. The most popular are dwarf cultivars not much more than 4–6 in (10–15 cm) tall. Flowers may be red, pink or white and foliage bright green, bronze or purple.

Propagation *Seed sown in late winter at a warm temperature of about 60–65°F (16–18°C) is the usual method. Prick off the very tiny seedlings when they have about three leaves.*

Soil *Ordinary, well-drained but not dry soil is satisfactory, ideally fortified with extra organic matter such as peat or leaf-mold.*

Position *Sun or half-day shade is suitable, some shade being desirable in areas of hot summers. Shelter from strong winds is necessary.*

Cultivation *Young plants should not be set outside until fear of frost has passed and the weather has warmed up.*

The tiny seedlings of begonia are difficult to manipulate with the fingers. Take a small plastic or wood label and cut a V-shaped notch in the end. Transfer the seedlings from the seed pot or pan to the pricking-off container, using the label as a tool.

Brachycome iberidifolia

Brachycome

The 75 species in this genus are found in North America, Africa, Australia and New Zealand, a curiously scattered distribution. One annual from Western Australia is widely cultivated. This is *B. iberidifolia*, the Swan River daisy, a slender branched plant to about 1 ft (30 cm) or more in height. It has a froth of very finely cut foliage and a profusion of fragrant blue daisy-like flowers about 1¼ in (3 cm) wide, from summer through fall. There are pink and white flowered selections. This daisy looks good in a mixed or shrub border.

Propagation *Seed is the only means. This is best sown in mid-spring at a warm temperature of not less than 60°F (16°C). Alternatively, sow seeds where the plants are to grow in late spring around the time of the last likely frost.*
Soil *Ordinary, well-drained but not dry soil of moderate fertility is suitable.*
Position *A sunny site is required for sturdy, long-flowering plants. Hot humid conditions are not appreciated.*
Cultivation *Young plants benefit if the growing tips are pinched out when they are about 2½ in (6 cm) tall. Although reasonably hardy, they should not be set outside until fear of frost has passed.*

Although young plants of B. iberidifolia branch naturally, attractively compact specimens will result if tips are pinched. When each plantlet is 2–2½ in (5–6 cm) tall, remove the extreme tip with the nails of thumb and forefinger, then remove the tips of subsequent branches that form.

Briza maxima

Briza

The 20 or so annuals and perennials in this genus are popularly known as quaking grasses. *B. maxima* is an elegant plant popular with flower arrangers and useful to add contrast to a planting of more colorful annuals. A native of Mediterranean regions, it grows 16–24 in (40–60 cm) tall, larger or smaller depending on the richness of the soil. At first, each plant is like a broad-leaved grass, then up to a dozen or more erect stems arise, each topped by an airy cluster of pendent spikelets which tremble on thread-like stems. Individual spikelets are about ¾ in (2 cm) long and rather like silvery-green, purple-tinted lockets. This grass makes a splendid foil for the more brightly colored annuals. Try it with the hot red of *Salvia splendens*, for example, or the bright yellow of *Tagetes* sp. and the bright orange-yellow of *Eschscholzia californica*. *B. maxima* also combines with and enhances flowers of more gentle hues, such as species of *Clarkia*, *Nigella* and *Moluccella*.

Propagation *Seed is the only means of increase and is best sown thinly on site in spring. In mild winter areas, sow in early fall.*
Soil *A wide range of soil types is tolerated, though the poorer sorts should be enriched with fertilizer or organic matter.*
Position *A sunny site is required for the best results but a little shade will be tolerated.*
Cultivation *Thin out seedlings when young to encourage sturdy, many-stemmed plants.*

Browallia speciosa

Browallia

Two of the six species in this genus are valuable pot plants for the home and greenhouse and also make a fine display in the summer garden. *B. speciosa major* from Colombia has the largest flower. It is really a shrubby perennial to 3 ft (90 cm) or more, but grown as an annual seldom exceeds 1½–2 ft (45–60 cm). Its rich, purple-blue flowers are about 2 in (5 cm) wide and are borne in succession until the first severe frost. *B.s.m.* 'Alba', Silver Bells , is white. *B. viscosa* is smaller in all its parts and seldom exceeds 1 ft (30 cm) in height while *B.v.* 'Sapphire' is half this and very compact.

Propagation *Seed sown in mid-spring in a warm temperature (65–70°F, 18–21°C) is the primary method. In frost-free climates, seed may be sown direct in the open garden.*

Soil *Fertile, well-drained but reasonably moist soil is the ideal, but ordinary garden soil is satisfactory.*

Position *A sunny site is best, though light shade is tolerated. In cool summer climates, a sheltered place will produce the best results.*

Cultivation *Plants of* B. speciosa *will be bushier if the tips are pinched out when about 4 in (10 cm) tall and then placed in 3–4 in (7.5–10 cm) pots.*

If containers more than 6 in (15 cm) deep are used for seed-sowing, it is advisable to add drainage material before filling with soil. Place pieces of broken pot, tile or slate over all cracks and holes wider than ½ in (1 cm), then cover this with 1 in (2.5 cm) of rough peat or potting mix sievings. Fill up with potting or seed-sowing mix and firm in the usual way.

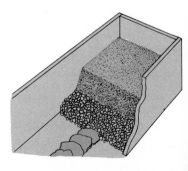

Calendula officinalis

Calendula

The common pot marigold, *C. officinalis*, is still one of the main standbys of the annual garden. It is not known in the wild and probably evolved from the European field marigold, *C. arvensis*. Although it can live for up to two years, it is best treated as an annual. The daisy-like flower-heads can be 2–3 in (5–7.5 cm) wide and come in bright shades of pale yellow to rich orange. Double-flowered cultivars are bigger and more popular. They range in height from 1 ft (30 cm) to 20 in (50 cm).

Propagation *Seeds are the only means, sown in spring where they are to grow. Earlier-flowering plants can be achieved by sowing a month sooner indoors.*
Soil *Well-drained but not dry soil of moderate fertility is best. Too rich a medium will produce lush, leafy plants at the expense of flowers.*
Position *A sunny site is preferred but light shade is tolerated, especially in areas with hot summers.*
Cultivation *If young plants get leggy, pinch out their tips to promote bushiness. Faded flower heads must be regularly removed to prolong the blooming season.*

Ray floret seed

The 'petals' of a marigold are technically known as ray florets, each one a tiny flower in its own right with all the petals fused into one. Disk florets, which form the center of the semi-double flower head shown here, have very tiny separate petals. Ray florets produce large, spiny, 'C'-shaped seeds; disk florets smaller, smoother ones.

Callistephus chinensis

Callistephus

China aster, *C. chinensis*, from east Asia is an elegant, blue-purple, yellow-centered daisy to about 2½ ft (80 cm). In cultivation it has proved highly mutable and a very wide range of heights, flower forms and colors are available. The cultivars can be grouped according to their flowers, most of which are double. The Ball group has rounded flower heads of quilled petals; Chrysanthemum and Peony-flowered bear flowers resembling those of the plants for which they are named; Ostrich Plume has long, waved petals, and Spider long, slender quilled ones. Pompon, akin to Ball, has compact plants rarely above 1 ft (30 cm) high.

Propagation *Seed is the only means of increase and must be sown around mid-spring in a medium temperature of 55–60°F (13–16°C). Prick off the seedlings as soon as the first true or rough leaf shows.*
Soil *A moist but well-drained soil rich in organic matter is the ideal.*
Position *Although a little shade is tolerated, especially in regions of warm summers, these plants need plenty of sun.*
Cultivation *Young plants are frost tender and must not be put outside until the weather warms up. Weed regularly in the weeks after transplanting.*

Well-grown plants branch from near the base as shown here, but the overall habit can be loose or compact depending on the cultivar type. In general, the tall sorts, single and double-flowered, are fairly loose, the short cultivars very compact.

Campanula medium

Campanula

The Canterbury bells, *C. medium*, is one of the most popular biennials. This native of Italy and south-eastern France forms a handsome rosette of hairy, lance-shaped leaves up to 1 ft (30 cm) across in its first year. In the second year a rosette rises in the middle and a stem up to 3 ft (90 cm) or so forms. This branches in the upper part to produce an elongated dome of big bells, each about 2 in (5 cm) long, in shades of lilac-blue to purple, pink and white. In *C.m. calycanthema* each flower has a saucer-shaped, colored calyx.

Propagation *Seed is the only method and must be sown in a cold frame or the open ground in early summer.*
Soil *Well-drained but not dry soil, enriched with organic matter, is the ideal.*
Position *A sunny site is required but some morning or afternoon shade will be tolerated.*
Cultivation *Whether raised in pots, boxes or the open ground, the young plants must be grown in nursery rows set 1 ft (30 cm) apart in the first summer. Transplant them in the fall into the flowering site. In areas of severe winters, the plants need cold frame protection or a light mulch of hay or bracken.*

The cup-and-saucer flowers of C. medium calycanthema *arose long ago as a mutation (sport), which turned the margins of the green sepals into colored petal-like lobes forming a ring at the base of the bell.*

AMARANTHACEAE

Celosia argentea cristata

Celosia

Only the tropical Asian *C. argentea* in this genus of 60 species is widely cultivated. The botanical name will seldom, if ever, be found in seed lists, however, as it primarily refers to the wild plant which has silvery-white flowers. From it have developed two widely different plants, *C.a. cristata plumosa*, the Prince of Wales feathers, and *C.a. cristata*, the cockscomb. The latter is a mutant (sport) in which all flowering branches have been condensed into a heavily convoluted fan or, more fancifully, a cockscomb. The Plumosa cultivars range from 1–3 ft (30–90 cm) but the Cristatas seldom exceed 1 ft (30 cm).

Propagation *Seed, sown in mid-spring at a warm temperature of about 70°F (21°C), is the only means.*
Soil *Well-drained but moist, moderately rich soil gives the best results.*
Position *A sunny site sheltered from strong winds is essential in cool summer areas. Elsewhere, a little shade is tolerated.*
Cultivation *This plant is of tropical origin and must not be set outside until fear of frost has passed and the weather warms up. The young plants must be fed and are best grown in 3–4 in (7.5–10 cm) pots until planted out.*

The plume-like flower clusters of this species, commonly called the Prince of Wales feathers, may seem far removed from the cockscomb illustrated above but it represents the basic wild form of C. argentea, *though in brighter colors than the truly wild plant. Tall forms can exceed 3 ft (90 cm) and make elegant pot plants or focal points in a bedding scheme.*

Centaurea cyanus

Centaurea

Although mainly composed of perennials, the best known member of this genus is undoubtedly *C. cyanus*, the annual cornflower. Formerly a grain-crop weed of south-eastern Europe, it is an erect plant to 3 ft (90 cm) tall. The original species has flowers with a single ring of outer petals (florets) but modern strains from seedsmen have fuller blooms in shades of blue, purple, red, pink and white. There are also dwarf forms, known as 'Polka Dot', to 1 ft (30 cm) in height. Equally decorative is *C. moschata*, Sweet Sultan, a 2 ft (60 cm) plant with much larger, fragrant flowers in yellow, red-purple, pink and white.

Propagation *Sow seeds where they are to grow in spring. Alternatively, sow earlier but under cover. In mild winter areas, seed sown in the fall will produce finer plants.*

Soil *Ordinary garden soil is suitable, ideally with added organic matter if very sandy or on the poor side.*

Position *A sunny site is the ideal for this annual, though a little morning or afternoon shade is tolerated.*

Cultivation *Seedlings must be thinned promptly and kept regularly weeded. Any checks to early growth will reduce the display of flowers. In windy sites, support plants with twiggy sticks.*

Stretch black cotton thread over sown seed or seedlings to discourage birds. It is important to use cotton, which snaps fairly readily, and not a stronger man-made thread which can trap or strangle a bird.

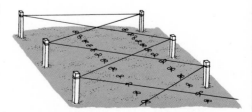

Cheiranthus Cheiri

Cheiranthus

In mild winter areas, *C. Cheiri*, the common wallflower, is a popular spring bedding plant, particularly in parks and public gardens. A native of the eastern Mediterranean region and widely naturalized elsewhere, the wild plant is a short-lived, shrubby perennial. Modern seed strains are less long-lived and are always grown as biennials. They are also larger flowered and embrace a much wider color range, including red-brown, blood-red, deep and pale yellow, ivory and rosy-salmon. The average height range of the various cultivars is 15–18 in (38–45 cm) but there is a dwarf race at about 10 in (25 cm).

Propagation *Seed is the primary method, sown in frames or the open ground in summer. Double-flowered cultivars are raised from summer cuttings.*
Soil *Ordinary soil is suitable but it must be well-drained and, ideally, alkaline. Acid soil should be dressed with lime.*
Position *A sunny site is necessary but a little morning or afternoon shade is tolerated. In cold areas a sheltered site is advisable.*
Cultivation *Young plants must be grown in nursery rows and transplanted to the flowering site in the fall. In severe winter areas, grow plants in frames and plant out in spring.*

Orange-yellow and sometimes mahogany-red are the colors of wild wallflower plants. During the centuries of cultivation, however, different colors have developed as mutations and plant breeders have used them to create further shades, including white, scarlet, crimson, salmon and purple.

Chrysanthemum carinatum

Chrysanthemum

Among the 200 species in this genus are three annuals which have much to offer the gardener. All are about 2 ft (60 cm) tall, with gaily colored daisy flowers 2 in (5 cm) or more wide. Showiest is *C. carinatum*, the 'tricolor chrysanthemum', which has purple disks with yellow-based white or red ray petals, strikingly banded in red, maroon or purple. *C. coronarium*, the crown daisy, has yellow disked flowers with golden yellow to white rays. Modern seed strains are often hybrids between the two species. *C. segetum*, corn marigold, has yellow to white daisies and distinctive gray-green leaves.

Propagation *Seed is the only means and can be sown either on site in spring or before this under cover for an earlier display.*

Soil *Reasonably fertile soil is needed for the best results; ordinary soil must be enriched with organic matter.*

Position *A sunny site is best but a little shade is tolerated and can be beneficial in areas of hot summers.*

Cultivation *Seedlings should be thinned with care and kept free of weeds. Give water during dry spells, especially in the early stages. Remove faded flower heads promptly to prolong the display.*

Well-grown, vigorous plants of C. carinatum *form bushy plants that almost resemble small shrubs. When in full bloom, they add substance and distinction to any bed or border of annuals.*

Clarkia amoena

Clarkia

This genus has now been united by botanists with *Godetia*, and so contains some of the most popular annuals. All the cultivated species and cultivars have a showy elegance, grow rapidly and are easy to please. Best known are *C. pulchella* and *C. unguiculata* (*C. elegans*), both about 1½ ft (45 cm) tall with mostly pompon-like flowers in shades of red, pink, purple and white. *C. amoena Whitneyi* has larger, broader-petalled flowers. There is a dwarf strain to 10 in (25 cm) tall.

Propagation *Seed is the only method, usually sown on site in spring. In areas of hot, humid summers, sow in early spring under glass so that plants bloom before the heat becomes too great.*
Soil *Ordinary soil is suitable if well-drained but not dry. Rich soil will promote foliage at the expense of flowers.*
Position *A sunny site is needed in cool summer areas. Elsewhere, a little morning or afternoon shade is tolerated.*
Cultivation *Seedlings must be kept free of weeds and thinned with care. In windy sites in particular, some sort of support is advisable.*

This is the typical double-flowered clarkia. Usually sold as C. elegans, *it is correctly* C. unguiculata *and a native of California.*

Cleome Hasslerana

Cleome

So distinctive is this genus of 150 tropical annuals and shrubs that some botanists place it in a family of its own, the *Cleomaceae*. Only one annual is widely grown, *C. Hasslerana*, which is often listed by seedsmen as *C. pungens* or *C. spinosa*. Colloquially known as spider flower, it is a slender plant 3–4 ft (90–120 cm) tall. The fingered leaves are rich green, slightly sticky and aromatic and make an attractive foil for the spikes of pink or white flowers, which are composed of four stalked petals inclined upwards, several very long stamens and a curious stalked ovary.

Propagation *Seed is the only means, sown in early to mid-spring at a warm temperature of about 65°F (18°C).*
Soil *Well-drained but not dry soil of moderate fertility is needed. Poorer soils should be enriched with organic matter.*
Position *A sunny site is required though in hot summer areas light shade is tolerated. Shelter from strong winds is advisable.*
Cultivation *Young plants are tender and must not be set outside until all fear of frost has passed and the weather has warmed up. They do best if grown in 4 in (10 cm) pots prior to planting out.*

Well-grown specimens of C. Hasslerana *can reach 3–4 ft (90–120 cm) in height and have an almost shrub-like quality. It is a splendid plant for the back of a border and an isolated group makes an attractive focal point.*

Consolida regalis

Consolida

T his generic name will be unfamiliar to most gardeners but it is now used by botanists to cover all the annual delphiniums, including those known as larkspurs. Two species provide the best known larkspurs, *C. ambigua* (*Delphinium Ajacis*) and *C. regalis* (*Delphinium Consolida*). The first is known vernacularly as rocket larkspur and has long spikes of blue, purple, pink and white flowers. *C. regalis* is similar but branches more freely and has shorter spikes. Both have finely dissected leaves and have given rise to double-flowered strains.

Propagation *Seed is the only means, sown on site as soon as soil conditions allow. In mild winter areas, sowing in the fall is recommended as this results in earlier flowers on finer plants.*
Soil *Ordinary well-drained soil of moderate fertility is the ideal. Poor soils should be enriched with organic matter.*
Position *A sunny site is essential, especially in the cooler summer areas.*
Cultivation *Young plants must be thinned with care and kept free of weeds. Water in dry spells, support the plants on windy sites.*

Many tall annuals need some sort of support, especially in exposed sites. The frame shown here is easily positioned when the plants are young. Later, when leaves grow through it, the support will be covered and will not detract from the floral effect.

Coreopsis tinctoria

Coreopsis

The vernacular name, tickseed, for this large genus of the daisy family refers to the insect-like appearance of the seeds. Two annual members are often grown to provide bright summer color. *C. tinctoria*, still often listed by seedsmen as *Calliopsis*, is the most frequently seen. Growing to about 2 ft (60 cm), it has narrowly cut leaves and yellow, purple-brown or parti-colored flowers to 1½ in (4 cm) wide. *C. basalis* (*C. drummondii*) is similar but usually a little shorter and with broader lobed leaves. The flowers tend to be larger, up to 2 in (5 cm) wide, with rich yellow, mahogany-centered flowers. As in *C. tinctoria* there are strains with varying amounts of chestnut-brown on the petals, some double or almost so. The seeds are more obviously 'bug-like', being narrowly pear-shaped; those of *C. tinctoria* are narrowly oblong. Both species are particularly attractive when grown in informal drifts at the front of a shrub or mixed border, perhaps filling in a gap left by spring bulbs.

Propagation *Seed is the only means, sown on site in spring once the weather starts to warm up. An earlier sowing under cover will flower sooner. In mild winter areas, sowing can be undertaken in the fall.*

Soil *Ordinary, well-drained but not dry soil is suitable. Too rich a medium will produce gross plants and few flowers.*

Position *A sunny site is required, though in hot summer areas a little shade is tolerated.*

Cultivation *Young plants must be kept weeded, and watered during dry spells.*

Cosmos bipinnatus

Cosmos

This generic name is derived from the Greek *kosmos*, meaning ornamental. No name could be more apt for the popular annual species
C. bipinnatus. Up to 3 ft (90 cm) or more in height, this slenderly
graceful plant has a wiry strength and usually stands up to winds
surprisingly well. The leaves are finely dissected and of fern-like deli-
cacy. The flowers, not typically daisy-like, have only eight very large
broad ray petals in shades of purple, crimson, pink and white. There are
cultivars with semi-double flowers. *C. sulphureus* has coarser foliage and
yellow to orange flowers.

Propagation *Seeds are the only means and must be sown around mid-spring in
a warm temperature (60–65°F, 16–18°C). In warm summer areas, seed can be
sown on site once fear of frost has passed and the weather has warmed.*
Soil *Ordinary garden soil is suitable, if moderately fertile but not rich; other
soils will produce over-leafy, poorly flowering plants.*
Position *A sunny site is essential for sturdy plants.*
Cultivation *Young plants must be kept free of weeds and watered during dry
spells. In very windy sites some light supports may be needed.*

C. sulphureus *adds shades of yellow
and orange to the color range provided
by* C. bipinnatus. *The cultivars
available mostly have semi-double
flower-heads, as shown here, borne on
stems rarely above 2 ft (60 cm).*

Cynoglossum amabile

Cynoglossum

The species *C. amabile*, Chinese forget-me-not, is one of those plants that can be grown as an annual or a biennial. However, it is a much finer plant if grown as a biennial, though it will only survive in mild winters. At first a rosette develops composed of softly hairy, gray-green leaves to 8 in (20 cm) long. At blooming time a sheaf of stems to 2 ft (60 cm) arises, each bearing many small branches and flowers like those of a large forget-me-not. The display usually extends into early fall.

Propagation *Seed is the only means. As a biennial, sow outside from early to mid-summer; when used as an annual, sow in early spring in a temperature of about 60°F (16°C).*

Soil *A fertile, well-drained but not dry soil is needed. Poorer soils should be enriched with organic matter.*

Position *A sunny site is best, especially in cool summer areas, though a little morning or afternoon shade is tolerated.*

Cultivation *As a biennial, the young plants must be grown on in nursery rows until the fall. In cold winter areas, they can be grown in frames and planted out in spring.*

A large plant of C. amabile *branches from the base and makes a fine bushy specimen with great impact in the annual border. This is an annual which does not look out of place among hardy perennials and can be used to fill gaps.*

Dahlia × hybrida

Dahlia

Considering its limited ancestry, the perennial dahlia is among the most variable of all popular garden plants for there are thousands of cultivated varieties in a wide range of colors and flower forms. Individual blooms may be single and daisy-like, or semi- or fully-double in a variety of ways. For convenience they are classified into groups: Cactus, with long, quilled florets; Ball, having short rolled florets densely packed into small rounded blooms; and Colarette, with a single row of large outer florets and a smaller inner row, sometimes in a contrasting color. All can be grown as annuals.

Propagation *The smaller dahlias, often grown as annuals, can be raised from seed sown in early spring at a warm temperature of 60°F (16°C). Raise all other cultivars from cuttings of young shoots (which arise from the 'eyes' on tubers) in spring or from tubers held over from the previous year.*
Soil *Well-drained but not dry, fertile soil is essential. Poor soils must be liberally mixed with organic matter.*
Position *A sunny site with some shade in the morning is advisable.*
Cultivation *Young plants must not be set outside until fear of frost has passed and the weather warmed up. Securely stake tall growing cultivars.*

To take dahlia cuttings, start tubers into growth in moist peat at 60°F (16°C) in early spring. When shoots are about 3 in (7.5 cm), remove just below a joint and insert in a cuttings mix and keep in a propagating case or plastic bag at 65°F (18°C).

Dianthus chinensis 'Heddewigii'

Dianthus

This genus is renowned for the carnation and pink but it also contains some first-rate rock and alpine species as well as the indispensable sweet William, *D. barbatus*, and the rainbow pink, *D. chinensis*. Both are really short-lived perennials but are always grown either as annuals or biennials. Sweet Williams have broadly lance-shaped, rich green leaves and small flowers in compact, flattened heads about 4 in (10 cm) wide. The spicily fragrant flowers are in shades of red, pink, purple and white, some strikingly bicolored. They range from almost 2 ft (60 cm) down to 6 in (15 cm) in height.

Propagation *Seeds of annuals must be sown in early spring at a warm temperature of about 60°F (16°C), those of biennials in summer.*
Soil *Well-drained and moderately fertile soil is needed. Over-rich soil will encourage leafy growth at the expense of flowers.*
Position *A sunny site is necessary, though a little shade is tolerated.*
Cultivation *Sweet Williams are usually grown as biennials, but annual seed strains are available. Grow biennial forms in a nursery bed or an open cold frame. In mild winter areas, they are best set out in the fall but in severe winter areas protect them in frames and plant out in spring. Plant out annual seedlings when all fear of frost has passed.*

Grown as a biennial, the sweet William (far left) sends up a substantial sheaf of stems to 2 ft (60 cm) in height. Indian or Chinese pink (left) is invariably grown as a dwarf bushy annual under the name D. chinensis 'Heddewigii' and such selected seed strain names as 'Baby Doll' and 'Magic Charms'.

Digitalis purpurea

Digitalis

Although there are 26 species in this genus, only one, *D. purpurea*, the common foxglove, is widely cultivated. This native of south-western Europe is one of the best known biennials, almost equalling *Campanula medium* in popularity. It is a splendid filler for informal situations, among shrubs, for example, or beneath a light tree cover. The typically one-sided spikes of thimble-shaped bells rise to an average height of 4 ft (1.2 m). In rich soil they can be much taller. The 'Excelsior' strain is more robust, with the flowers evenly arranged all round the stem. Flower color varies from white to red-purple, with or without spots. In English folklore, the foxglove was a fairy's or goblin's plant, no doubt from the curious shape and size of the flower and the poisonous nature of the plant (it contains the heart stimulant digitalin). On light soils, the abundantly produced tiny seeds self-sow and can be a nuisance, so it is wise to cut down spent flower spikes.

Propagation *Seed is the only means. Sow in a frame in early summer.*
Soil *Ordinary soil that is well drained but not dry is suitable.*
Position *Partial shade is the ideal, either dappled as beneath trees or with half day light in deeper shade.*
Cultivation *Young plants need to be grown on in a nursery bed and must be kept regularly weeded and watered. In mild winter areas, set them out in their winter quarters in the fall but in severe winter areas protect them in frames until the following spring.*

Dimorphotheca sinuata

Dimorphotheca

This South African genus of tender annuals and perennials contains some colorfully elegant, daisy-flowered plants, sometimes referred to as cape marigolds. *D. pluvialis*, often listed as *D. annua*, is a spreading to erect species about 1 ft (30 cm) tall, with narrow leaves and 2–2½ in (5–6 cm) wide daisies. The daisies have white, purple-backed ray florets surrounding a golden-brown, blue-tinted disk. *D. sinuata* is also known as *D. calendulacea*. It has narrower leaves and slightly taller stems, bearing flowers with steely blue disks and yellow to white ray florets. Some seed strains are hybrids between the two and have a wider color range.

Propagation *Seed is the only means. It can be sown on site in late spring but is best sown earlier under cover in a warm temperature of about 60°F (16°C).*
Soil *A well-drained soil is essential, ideally moderately fertile but not rich.*
Position *Sunshine is essential as the flowers open only in sunny weather. They do not thrive in regions where summers are both hot and humid.*
Cultivation *Young plants must not be set outside until fear of frost has passed and must then be kept free of weeds until established.*

Once seedling annuals appear, they must be kept regularly weeded. Failure to do this can result in their becoming smothered thus inhibiting their growth. Use a small onion hoe or similar hand tool so that there is no damage to the seedlings.

Eschscholzia californica

Eschscholzia

The popular and brilliant California poppy, *E. californica*, is technically a short-lived perennial but performs best as an annual. It is a
tufted plant about 1 ft (30 cm) in height, with finely dissected gray-
green leaves, which are decorative in themselves. The four-petalled
orange to yellow flowers have a satiny luster which makes them appear
to shine with a light of their own. There are semi-double seed strains
which contain other colors, including pink and carmine. Generally
smaller and with even more finely-cut leaves in *E. caespitosa* (*E.
tenuifolia*), one of the few annuals not out of place in a rock garden.

Propagation *Seed is the only means; sow on site when the weather warms in
spring. For an early display, sow seeds in groups of three to four in 3 in (7.5 cm)
pots under cover in early to mid-spring.*
Soil *Well-drained soil is essential, even when it is fairly poor. Rich soil
encourages foliage at the expense of flowers.*
Position *Full sun is needed for a good display, though a little shade in the
morning or afternoon is tolerated.*
Cultivation *Young plants do not transplant well and must be thinned out with
care to the required spacing.*

The species E. californica
*is now available in an
increased color range thanks
to sporting and the skill of
plant breeders. There are
also semi-double flowered
selections (right) and those
with charmingly crimped
petals (far right).*

Felicia amelloides

Felicia

No other member of the daisy family can compete with this genus when it comes to providing pure blue flowers. *F. Bergerana* has acquired the vernacular name kingfisher daisy from the deep blue color of its ray florets. It is a true annual to about 8 in (20 in) tall, with small, narrowly oblong leaves and a bushy habit. The blue daisy or marguerite, *F. amelloides*, sometimes listed as *Agathaea coelestis*, is a small shrubby perennial 1 ft (30 cm) or more in height, with oval leaves and sky blue flowers. Raised annually from seed or cuttings, it behaves as an annual. If desired it can be carefully dug up at the end of the season, potted and brought into a sunny window where it will continue to flower for some time. Both *F. Bergerana* and *F. amelloides* make splendid edging plants to a formal planting of annuals. They can also be used as ground cover beneath taller annuals.

Propagation *Sow true annuals in a warm temperature (about 60°F, 16°C) in early or mid-spring. Perennials can be grown from seed or increased from cuttings taken from over-wintered plants in spring.*
Soil *A well-drained soil of only moderate fertility is essential.*
Position *A sunny site is necessary as the flowers open fully only in direct light. These plants do not appreciate areas where the summers are both hot and very humid.*
Cultivation *Young plants must not be set outside until all fear of frost has passed and the weather is warming up.*

Gaillardia pulchella

Gaillardia

Only two out of the 28 known species in this genus are cultivated. Both are North American perennials which can be grown as annuals or biennials and both are known as blanket flower. *G. aristata* can reach 2 ft (60 cm) tall, but is usually somewhat less. It has gray-green, lance-shaped leaves and flower heads 2½–3 in (6–7.5 cm) wide, composed of a brownish-purple disk and broad, yellow ray florets, sometimes with purple-red bases. *G. pulchella* is similar but shorter, with ray florets entirely red-purple or with small, yellow tips. Seed strains are often hybrids between the two.

Propagation *To get plants in bloom the first year, seed must be sown in early to mid-spring in a warm temperature of about 60°F (16°C). Alternatively, sow in early summer in nursery rows and treat as biennials.*

Soil *Ordinary garden soil, well-drained but not dry, and moderately fertile is the ideal for these two species.*

Position *A sunny site should be chosen, though a little morning or afternoon shade is tolerated.*

Cultivation *Seedling plants should be thinned with care, kept regularly weeded and watered during dry spells. Support with twiggy sticks on windy sites.*

The typical daisy-like flower head of G. aristata *is much like that of the wild species but with some extra ray florets. The fully double forms are composed of greatly elongated disk florets, which give each flower-head an almost fluffy appearance like a pompon.*

Gomphrena globosa

Gomphrena

Globe amaranth (*G. globosa*) is the apt name of the only species in this genus to be widely grown. It is a bushy annual to about 1½ ft (45 cm) tall, with elliptic to oblong leaves, the largest being 4 in (10 cm) long. The flowers are carried in terminal, ovoid to globular heads. Each flower is minute and almost hidden by the larger, chaffy-textured, colored bract. Red-purple is the basic color but, in modern seed strains, orange, yellow, pink and white occur. The everlasting nature of the flower heads makes them useful for adding to winter arrangements of dried flowers.

Propagation *Seed is the only means of increase. For early flowering it must be sown in a warm temperature of about 60–65°F (16–18°C) in mid-spring, but a later display will result from sowing on site when all fear of frost has passed.*
Soil *Ordinary garden soil, providing it is well drained, is perfectly satisfactory. Even quite poor soil is acceptable, but one of moderate fertility is ideal.*
Position *For compact, free-flowering plants, a sunny site is essential.*
Cultivation *Young plants raised under cover must not be set outside until all fear of frost has passed.*

Seedlings of this species and those of other annuals are likely to suffer from damping-off disease if they are sown too thickly and watered too freely. Attacked seedlings wither at the base and topple over (left). Treatment with a suitable fungicide will halt the spread of disease.

Gypsophila elegans

Gypsophila

The airy grace of certain species in this genus, known as baby's-breath, has long been considered an ideal accompaniment to larger, brighter flowers. Both perennial and annual species are available and are generally grown for cut flowers. The annual species, notably *G. elegans*, is grown alongside other annuals for garden effect. For example, a drift of mixed *G. elegans* and *Anchusa capensis* (blue cornflowers) provides a beautiful sight. For variety, there are pink and carmine strains of gypsophila, for example 'Rosa' and 'Carminea'. The best white strain is 'Covent Garden'. All are best sown directly into the site where they will flower. Root disturbance tends to reduce vigor and total height and spread. The beauty and usefulness of gypsophila lies in the clouds of small white flowers and the bigger the plants the better the display.

Propagation *Seed is the only means. In mild areas, sow on site in the fall, to encourage free growth and early flowering. Elsewhere, sow in spring.*

Soil *A well-drained soil is essential; very limy soils are tolerated with equanimity.*

Position *A sunny site is best though a little shade in the morning or afternoon is acceptable.*

Cultivation *Seedlings must be thinned with care and kept free of weeds in the early stages. In windy sites, the support of twiggy sticks is advisable.*

Helianthus annuus

Helianthus

Most of the garden-worthy sunflowers are perennials but there are two highly decorative annuals, the cucumber-leaf sunflower, *H. debilis cucumerifolius*, and the common sunflower, *H. annuus*. The latter is one of the fastest growing and tallest of all annuals. It also has the largest flower heads, not only in its genus but in its family. Well grown plants can attain 10 ft (3 m) or more in height, with flower heads 1 ft (30 cm) wide. Cucumber-leaf sunflowers reach 6½ ft (2 m) and bear several yellow and red-brown daisies about 3 in (7.5 cm) wide. Both species have double-flowered cultivars.

Propagation *Seed is the only means and must be sown on site in spring when the weather warms up. Earlier flowering can be achieved by sowing singly in small pots in a warm temperature of about 60°F (16°C) a month earlier.*
Soil *For the biggest plants, a rich, moisture-retaining but well-drained soil is required. Poorer soils must be fortified with plenty of organic matter.*
Position *A sunny site is needed, though a little shade is tolerated.*
Cultivation *Water young plants during dry spells and keep them regularly weeded. Extra tall plants are prone to damage by strong winds so the use of stakes to avoid the stems snapping is advisable.*

Unlike most annuals, the giant sunflower seldom branches, but puts all its energy into one tall, robust stem and a solitary, often huge flower head. The black and white striped seeds yield an oil used in the manufacture of margarine and for cooking.

Helichrysum bracteatum monstrosum

Helichrysum

This genus contains one of the best known of all annual everlasting flowers, *H. bracteatum*. Commonly called strawflower, this native of Australia is represented in gardens by the large, semi-double flowered *H. b. monstrosum*. What appear to be petals or ray florets are actually hard textured, straw-like bracts, generally in shades of red, orange, yellow, pink or white. They usually grow to 2 ft (60 cm) or more but there is a dwarf strain reaching 1 ft (30 cm) or so. For drying, cut the stems just as the main flowers open, then tie them in small bunches and hang them in an airy, shady place. Although often cultivated purely for cutting and drying, modern strains of strawflower are well worth growing for their colorful display in the garden. They combine well with other members of the daisy family, such as *Chrysanthemum carinatum*, bedding dahlias, *Gaillardia* and *Zinnia*. They can also be used very effectively on their own with a backing of *Kochia*.

Propagation *Seed is the only means of propagation and should be sown in a warm temperature of about 60°F (16°C) in mid-spring. The young plants will become established more quickly if grown individually in 3–4 in (7.5–10 cm) pots, prior to planting out.*
Soil *A well-drained, moderately fertile soil is the best. Rich soils produce over leafy, soft plants that do not stand well.*
Position *A sunny site is necessary, particularly in areas with cool summers.*
Cultivation *Newly set out young plants must be watered during dry spells and kept free of weeds.*

BORAGINACEAE

Heliotropium arborescens

Heliotropium

Both the plant and the heavy scent of heliotrope, or cherry-pie, have long been favorites. Properly called *H. arborescens*, but also known as *H. peruvianum*, it is an evergreen shrub from Peru that can be grown from cuttings. There are also seed strains which flower the first summer after sowing. As a shrub it can attain 4 ft (1.2 m) in height but as an annual it rarely exceeds 1–1½ ft (30–45 cm). There are several cultivars in shades of lavender, violet, deep purple or white.

Propagation *Take cuttings from cut back, overwintered plants in spring or sow seeds in early spring. Keep both in a warm temperature of about 65°F (18°C).*
Soil *A fertile, moisture-retaining but well-drained soil is required, though poorer soils give reasonable results.*
Position *A sunny site is necessary, though a little shade is tolerated.*
Cultivation *Young plants must not be set outside until all fear of frost has passed and the weather starts to warm. Plants to be over-wintered must be lifted, potted and kept in a greenhouse at a minimum of 45–50°F (7–10°C).*

Grown as standards, these plants make good container specimens for a patio. Keep rooted cuttings growing vigorously by regularly potting on and applying fertilizer. Pinch out all side shoots. When the stem has reached the desired height, allow four more leaves to form and then pinch out the tip. Shoots from these upper leaf axils will form the head.

51

Helipterum roseu...

Helipterum

This Australian and South African genus is closely related t Helichrysum and bears similar, everlasting flowers. The two mai species grown in the garden are slender plants and much more graceful than those of *Helichrysum bracteatum*. *Helipterum roseum*, formerly *Acro linium roseum*, is the most familiar. It grows to 16 in (40 cm) or more in height with strong, wiry stems and small, slender, gray-green leaves The flower heads are bright pink or white, about 1½ in (4 cm) or mor in width. *H. manglesii* (*Rhodanthe manglesii*) has the same sort of flower but longer, broadly elliptic leaves.

Propagation *Seed is the only means of propagation. Sow thinly on site in spring. For earlier flowering sow under cover in a warm temperature of about 60°F (16°C), setting out the young plants when all fear of frost has passed.*
Soil *Well-drained, light soils are preferred but even fairly poor soils will produc worthwhile plants.*
Position *A sunny site is essential, especially in areas with cool summers.*
Cultivation *Young plants must be kept free of weeds. For drying, cut the stems as the top flowers open, tie in small bunches and hang in an airy, shaded place.*

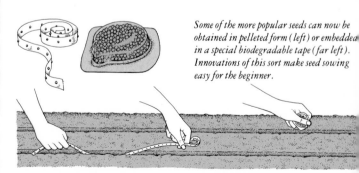

Some of the more popular seeds can now be obtained in pelleted form (left) or embedded in a special biodegradable tape (far left). Innovations of this sort make seed sowing easy for the beginner.

Iberis amara

Iberis

Although the common name candytuft can be used for all 30 members of this genus, it is the annual species to which it usually refers. *I. umbellata* is the best known, a branched plant to 1 ft (30 cm) or more, with four-petalled, pink to purple-red flowers in rounded, flattish clusters. It has narrowly lance-shaped leaves, which are only occasionally toothed. *I. amara*, also known as *I. coronaria*, has toothed or lobed leaves that broaden out towards the tips. The white to purplish flowers are borne in large clusters, which lengthen into spikes. They are also fragrant, whereas those of *I. umbellata* are not. Some seed strains are hybrids of the two.

Propagation *Seed is the only means of propagation and is usually sown on site in spring, once the weather starts to warm up. For an early display, it can be sown under cover a month sooner.*
Soil *Well-drained, moderately fertile soil is the ideal. Very poor soils must be given a dressing of organic fertilizer.*
Position *A sunny site is needed, though some shade is tolerated.*
Cultivation *Seedlings should be thinned and weeded with care and young plants watered during dry spells. Cut spent flower heads to prolong the display.*

Common or globe candytuft, I. umbellata, has flattened heads of flowers on a plant that branches more freely than the generally taller rocket candytuft, I. amara. In general, it is the best for sowing on site and is particularly useful for filling gaps left by spring bulbs.

Impatiens Wallerana

Impatiens

For many years busy Lizzie or patient Lucy (*I. Wallerana*) has been a favorite house plant. In recent years, seed strains of compact, early flowering cultivars have been developed to grow as annuals. These are available in shades of red, pink, purple, orange and white, some with strikingly bicolored petals. Long before *I. Wallerana* became a garden plant, the garden or rose balsam (*I. Balsamina*) added its charms to our summer gardens. Very different in appearance, it is an erect species, often with a single, very robust stem 1½–2 ft (45–60 cm) tall, crowded with lance-shaped leaves and lilac, pink, red, purple, yellow or white double flowers like tiny camellias.

Propagation I. Balsamina *grows only from seed but* I. Wallerana *can be raised from either seed or cuttings. Sow seed in early to mid-spring at a warm temperature of about 60–65°F (16–18°C) or take cuttings in spring from overwintered plants.*
Soil *Well-drained but moisture-retaining soil enriched with organic matter is the ideal, though reasonable results can be expected in ordinary soil.*
Position *In cool summer areas, a mainly sunny site is required. In warmer areas, up to half-day shade is tolerated.*
Cultivation *The young plants must not be set outside until all fear of frost has passed and the weather has warmed up.*

The rose or garden balsam,
I. Balsamina, has been cultivated
in gardens for almost 400 years.
Although a native of the tropical areas
of India, China and the Malay
Peninsula, it thrives in both warm and
cool summer regions.

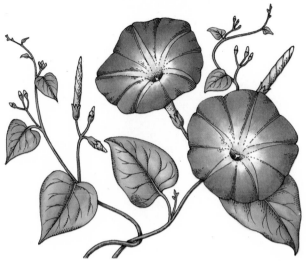

Ipomoea purpurea

Ipomoea

The annual climbing members of this genus are among the most gorgeous of all summer garden plants. Known as morning-glories, they climb by means of tightly twining stems and are ideal for covering and screening fences or walls. They can also be grown up a tripod or wigwam of sticks, when they make an excellent focal point in a bed or border of shorter plants. Best known is the common morning-glory (*I. purpurea*), with 2½ in (6 cm) long flowers in shades of blue, purple or pink. *I. tricolor* (*I. rubrocaerulea*) has larger, wider flowers of purple-blue or white while *I.t.* 'Heavenly Blue' has rich sky-blue flowers.

Propagation *Seed is the only means of increase: sow in mid-spring at a warm temperature of 70°F (21°C) or above. For best results, soak the seed for 12 hours in tepid water, then sow singly in 3 in (7.5 cm) pots.*
Soil *Moisture-retaining but well-drained, fertile soil is essential. Enrich poorer soils with organic matter and fertilizer.*
Position *A sunny site is necessary; some shade in the afternoon is tolerated.*
Cultivation *A support must be provided for the twining stems: vertical wires, strings, sticks or netting are best. Young plants must not be set out until all fear of frost has passed.*

The morning-glories are indeed among the most glorious of annual climbers but must have proper support to display their charms. Rigid plastic netting is useful, either flat or rolled into a cylinder, but a wigwam of canes or sticks provides the best support. Well covered with plants and flowers, it soon becomes the focus of the garden.

Kochia scoparia trichophylla

Kochia

At least 80 species are recorded in this genus, but only one is widely grown. This is the so-called burning bush or summer cypress, *K. scoparia*. The name burning bush is confusing as it has been applied to several plants, notably *Dictamnus albus* which gives off an ignitable volatile oil. The name has also been attached to *K. scoparia trichophylla* because the whole plant turns red in the fall. Summer cypress, on the other hand, is the most apt name for this annual, which looks like a dwarf coniferous tree 1½–2 ft (45–60 cm) in height, with slender, bright green leaves and totally insignificant flowers.

Propagation *Seed is the only means of propagation. Sow on site in late spring when the weather warms up. For earlier plants, sow a month before, under cover in a warm temperature of about 60–65°F (16–18°C).*
Soil *Well-drained, moderately fertile soil is the ideal.*
Position *A sunny site gives the best results, though a little morning or afternoon shade is acceptable.*
Cultivation *Young plants must be kept free of weeds, and watered during dry spells. If they branch only sparingly at first, pinch out the stem tips to encourage further branching.*

A well-grown plant of summer cypress can be remarkably dense and shrub-like and, indeed, mimics a miniature cypress. It makes a perfect foil for colorful summer flowers.

Lathyrus odoratus

Lathyrus

This genus includes only one annual plant, the sweet pea, *L. odoratus*. A climbing species, it is native to southern Italy and Sicily but has been changed out of all recognition by plant breeders. Well grown plants can reach or even exceed 8 ft (2.4 m), with robust winged stems and leaves composed of two narrow, gray-green leaflets and a branched tendril. The pea-shaped flowers are 1½–2 in (4–5 cm) wide and embrace almost every color in the rainbow. Some are of one color, others bicolored and picotee. There are dwarf growing sorts, including the non-climbing *L. o. nanellus*, for example 'Little Sweetheart'.

Propagation *Sow seeds on site in spring, or in the fall in mild areas. Or sow under cover in late winter at a medium temperature (55–60°F, 13–16°C).*
Soil *A moderately rich, moist but well-drained soil is needed for the best plants. Poor soils must be enriched with organic matter.*
Position *A sunny site is the ideal, though some shade is acceptable.*
Cultivation *Remove tips of young plants when they have two to three leaves to encourage strong basal shoots. For high quality blooms, retain only one stem, to channel the plant's energy into its blooms. Pinch out all tendrils and tie the stem to its support. Faded flowers should be removed regularly.*

The strongest stems of a sweet pea seedling come from the base, so pinch out the tip at two leaves to encourage their production (left). For quality flowers, restrict each plant to one basal stem, pinch out tendrils and side shoots and tie to its support (right).

Lavatera trimestris

Lavatera

The rose-mallow, *L. trimestris*, is one of the loveliest members of its genus. A bushy plant to 3 ft (90 cm) or more, it has some three to seven rounded lobed leaves that grow to about 2½ in (6 cm) long. From summer through fall it produces terminal clusters of five-petalled, widely funnel-shaped flowers of satiny pink. The clearest and brightest colored form is called 'Loveliness'. The newer 'Silver Cup' has rose-pink, darker veined petals with white shading in the center. 'Mont Blanc' is pure white and contrasts beautifully with the colored cultivars.

Propagation *Seed is the only means of propagation, sown on site in spring. Place two to three seeds at each planting station, then thin to one later.*
Soil *Moisture-retaining but well-drained, fertile soil is needed for the best plants. Enrich poorer soils with organic matter.*
Position *A sunny site is best, but up to a half day of shade is tolerated.*
Cultivation *Weed young plants carefully and water in dry spells. Pick off dead blossoms to help prolong the display. In windy sites, support is recommended.*

Well-grown plants of the rose-mallow can exceed 3 ft (90 cm) in height, with almost woody stem bases and a well-branched, shrub-like appearance. With its large hibiscus-like flowers and bold foliage, a solitary group makes a fine point of interest for the garden.

Limnanthes Douglasii

Limnanthes

Restricted in the wild to western North America, this genus contains one outstanding annual member, *L. Douglasii*, the meadow foam. It is a low, spreading plant with bright green, somewhat fleshy leaves and a profusion of 1 in (2.5 cm) wide, five-petalled flowers. In the typical plant, the flowers are yellow at the base and white around the top. In *L. D. sulphurea* they are wholly yellow and in *L. D. nivea* wholly white. In the rarely cultivated *L. D. rosea*, the petals are totally white with pink veins. Meadow foam is an excellent subject for the front of a border and is much favored by bees. Where winters are comparatively mild it is worth sowing some seed in late summer or early fall. The foliage will be a pleasing sight in winter and the plants flower splendidly in spring. Used in this way, meadow foam makes a good under-planting for such bulbs as tulips.

Propatation *Seed is the only means of propagation. It should be sown thinly in spring, or in the fall in areas with mild winters.*
Soil *A moisture-retaining but well-drained, fertile soil gives the best results, but acceptable plants will grow in quite poor sites.*
Position *A sunny site is best, particularly in cool summer regions but this plant does not thrive in hot, humid areas.*
Cultivation *Thin seedlings with care and keep them regularly weeded. Watering is advisable during dry spells. In many areas, self-sown seedlings occur regularly and in mild winter areas these will flower in spring.*

Limonium sinuatum

Limonium

This large genus provides several garden-worthy perennials and annuals. Two of the latter are outstanding, the best known being common statice, *L. sinuatum* from the Mediterranean region. It forms a rosette of waved and deeply lobed leaves, from the center of which arise a sheaf of winged stems to 1½ ft (45 cm) tall. Each stem is topped by branched clusters of tubular, chaffy flowers in a wide color range which dry well. Even more distinctive in appearance is *L. Suworowii*, sometimes listed under the generic name *Psylliostachys*. Of similar height, it has erect, fingered flower clusters of rose pink.

Propagation *Seed is the only means of propagation. Sow on site in spring but in cool summer areas these species are best raised under cover. Sow at a warm temperature of 60–65°F (16–18°C) and grow the young plants in 3–4 in (7.5–10 cm) pots prior to planting out.*
Soil *Moderately fertile, well-drained but not dry soil is needed.*
Position *A sunny site is required, especially in cooler summer areas.*
Cultivation *These plants are not frost hardy and young plants must not be set outside until the weather warms up.*

Unlike many annuals, the common statice forms a rosette of handsome, lobed leaves before flowering. A group of these rosettes makes a pleasing foil for the sheafs of flowering stems which arise later. Usually only seeds of mixed colors are readily available.

Linaria maroccana

Linaria

Toadflax is the common name for the many members of this genus. They are much like small-flowered versions of *Antirrhinum* and the two genera are closely related. Both have flowers with closed mouths that have to be forced open by pollinating insects. Those of toadflax have a long spur containing nectar, but those of *Antirrhinum* are spurless. *L. maroccana* is the commonly grown annual. It is a slender, graceful plant 1 ft (30 cm) or more in height, with very narrow leaves and flowers in shades of purple, red, blue, pink and yellow. The best strain is the dwarf, compact 'Fairy Bouquet'.

Propagation *Seed is the only means of propagation. Sow on site in spring, or a few weeks earlier if under cover.*
Soil *Well-drained but otherwise ordinary soil is quite satisfactory. Too rich a soil will produce lush, floppy plants at the expense of flowers.*
Position *A sunny site is needed, though a little shade in the morning or afternoon is tolerated.*
Cultivation *The seedlings are very small and must be thinned with care and kept regularly weeded. In windy sites, the support of twiggy sticks is advisable.*

Violet-purple is the basic color of L. maroccana, *but there are now also shades of blue, red, pink, white and yellow. Single color seed selections are rarely available.*

Linum grandiflorum

Linum

This genus contains the commercial flax plant, *L. usitatissimum*, a dwarf form of which is also grown in flower gardens. An erect plant to about 15 in (38 cm) tall, it has narrow, gray-green leaves and pure blue, saucer-shaped flowers each with five petals. More often listed by seedsmen is the scarlet flax, *L. grandiflorum* 'Rubrum'. This has green leaves and slender stems to about 1 ft (30 cm) in height. The 1¼–1½ in (3–4 cm) wide flowers are bright red. These flaxes look well together, while separately they associate most effectively with gypsophila and other white-flowered plants.

Propagation *Seed is the only means of propagation. It should be sown thinly on site in spring or, in mild winter areas, in the fall. Alternatively, an early spring sowing can be made under cover at a medium temperature of about 55–60°F (13–16°C).*
Soil *Ordinary but well-drained soil of moderate fertility is the ideal.*
Position *For sturdy plants a sunny site is necessary, though where sunshine averages are high a little shade is tolerated.*
Cultivation *Seedlings must be thinned carefully and kept regularly weeded. They will also benefit from watering during dry spells.*

A flax plant has very slender stems and narrow leaves, which give it a light and airy appearance. Though slim, the stems are strong and flax seldom needs staking against strong winds.

Lobelia Erinus

Lobelia

Comparatively few of the 375 species in this genus are cultivated, but those that are deserve a place in most gardens. One outstanding perennial grown as an annual is *L. Erinus* from South Africa. It is much used for edging, particularly in association with summer bedding plants, but looks best when used in more informal settings. It can be particularly effective planted in drifts to cover gaps left by spring bulbs. 'Crystal Palace' is one of the most popular strains. In addition to the dark and light blue cultivars, there are those with purple, carmine or white blooms. All are spreading in habit but they rarely exceed 6 in (15 cm) in height.

Propagation *Seed is the usual method of propagation, although overwintered plants can be divided or used for cuttings in spring. Sow seed thinly, ideally mixed with several volumes of dry sand to aid even dispersal, and keep in a warm temperature of about 60–65°F (16–18°C).*
Soil *Moisture-retaining but well-drained soil is the ideal, but lobelia will grow well in ordinary soil.*
Position *A site in sun or partial shade is acceptable, though full sun is best in areas with cool summers.*
Cultivation *The seedlings are minute and it is standard practice to prick them off in small groups of three or four.*

The best lobelia for hanging baskets is the trailing species, L. tenuior *from Western Australia (right). It produces lax stems to 1 ft (30 cm) or more in length, which bear a succession of bright blue flowers. It contrasts greatly in habit with* L. Erinus *(far right).*

Lobularia maritima

Lobularia

In seed catalogs, the one popular member of this genus is still listed under *Alyssum* and is coloquially known as sweet alyssum. Botanically it is *L. maritima*, a seaside annual from southern Europe. Rarely above 6 in (15 cm) tall and of spreading habit, it has narrow leaves and numerous heads of tiny, four-petalled, fragrant white flowers. Modern cultivars tend to be shorter and much more compact, some with pink, purple or red flowers. Although frequently used for edging beds and borders, they are also effective in informal drifts as summer ground cover to fill gaps left by spring blooming bulbs. In a more formal situation sweet alyssum can be used to surround small groups or solitary plants of taller annuals, such as cornflower, *Cosmos*, *Salpiglossis*, *Scabiosa atropurpurea* and *Zinnia*. The smaller cultivars are useful for window boxes and can be used to fill temporary gaps in the rock garden.

Propagation *Seed is the only method of propagation. Sow on site in early spring, or in mild winter areas, sow in the fall for late spring flowering. To provide immediate cover for areas occupied by spring bulbs, sow seed earlier under cover and plant the seedlings out when bulb leaves appear.*
Soil *Sweet alyssum will grow in almost any soil which is moderately well drained; it thrives in dryish, limy situations.*
Position *A sunny site is best but a little shade is tolerated, especially in hot summer areas.*
Cultivation *Seedlings must be thinned with care and kept regularly weeded.*

Lunaria annua

Lunaria

Honesty, or moonwort, is the best known member of this small genus. Although a biennial, its Latin name is now *L. annua* though it was for long listed as *L. biennis*. It is a robust plant, forming a tuft of heart-shaped leaves in the first year, 6 in (15 cm) or more tall. In the second spring, generally a solitary stem grows up to 3 ft (90 cm) or more, carrying branched clusters of four-petalled, red-purple to white flowers. Oval, 1¼–2½ in (3–6 cm) flat pods develop later. When ripe, these split to release the seed, and reveal silvery-white membranes or 'moons' that are useful for winter flower arrangements.

Propagation *Seed is the only means of propagation. Sow in nursery rows in early summer. If seeding plants are left, self-sown seedlings often appear.*
Soil *Almost any soil is suitable though the plants will develop best in a humus-rich, moist but not wet soil.*
Position *Although full sun is tolerated, honesty is a woodland plant and thrives best in partial or dappled shade.*
Cultivation *Young plants are usually grown on in nursery rows and then planted into permanent sites in the fall or early spring. In informal situations, plant seedlings directly into their flowering stations.*

The finest plants of honesty are seen in areas with warm winters. From late summer onwards, the tufts of boldly heart-shaped foliage are attractive and especially welcome in winter.

Malcolmia maritim

Malcolmia

Of more than 30 species in this Mediterranean to central Asia genus, only one is widely cultivated. This is *M. maritima*, th so-called Virginia stock. It is a useful little plant, growing and flower ing rapidly from seed. Seldom above 8 in (20 cm) tall, it has severa wiry stems bearing oval to oblong leaves that terminate in short spike of four-petalled flowers. Naturally variable, the flowers range from re to pink, purple, yellow and white. *M. maritima* makes an effectiv edging to beds and borders.

Propagation *Seed is the only means of propagation. Sow on site at six-weekly intervals in spring or fall. This guarantees a long succession of flowers.*
Soil *Almost any soil is suitable providing it is well drained, but rich soil produces lush, ungainly growth at the expense of flowers.*
Position *A sunny site is ideal, though a little morning or afternoon shade is tolerated. It does not thrive in hot, humid conditions.*
Cultivation *Seed is invariably sown too thickly and the crowded seedlings left to fight for survival. For this reason, thin them out to about 3 in (7.5 cm) apart to ensure adequate space for each plant.*

Because individual plants of **M.** maritima *are slender, small and rather insignificant they need to be grown* en masse *to have any garden effect. Being quick to mature, they make useful cover for areas occupied by spring flowering bulbs.*

Matthiola incana

Matthiola

The most popular species in this genus is *M. incana*, a short-lived perennial from the south-west coasts of Europe. Known commonly as stock, it is a variable plant in stature and behavior. Plant breeders have developed several strains, some of which behave as annuals and others as biennials. All are erect plants with gray-felted leaves and spikes of four-petalled, fragrant flowers in shades of purple, red, pink, yellow or white. Double-flowered strains are readily available and are now the most popular of all. Ten week stocks (so called because they flower for ten weeks) are the most widely grown annual strain.

Propagation *Seed is the usual means, sown in early to mid-spring at 60°F (16°C) for a summer flowering. For late summer and fall flowering, sowing is undertaken outside when the weather warms up in spring.*
Soil *Well-drained ordinary soil is suitable but these plants will thrive in the limiest of conditions.*
Position *A sunny site is needed, though in areas with very warm summers light morning or afternoon shade is tolerated. Hot, humid weather is not appreciated.*
Cultivation *Although reasonably hardy, young plants raised under cover should not be set out until fear of frost has passed.*

Basically a woody-stemmed perennial, the stock, more than any other plant grown as an annual or biennial, can take on the appearance of a small shrub. Not all the many kinds of stock behave in this way and to achieve a shrub shape Brompton or Perpetual flowering strains must be obtained.

Mentzelia Lindley

Mentzelia

About 60 species of annuals, biennials, perennials and shrubs com
prise this North and South American genus. Although several ar
attractive, only *M. Lindleyi*, which is also known as *Bartonia aurea*, i
widely grown. This native of California is about 1 ft (30 cm) in height
but sometimes taller under ideal conditions. It first forms a rosette o
deeply lobed, somewhat hoary, hairy leaves, then rapidly extend
upwards, branching as it does so. Every stem tip terminates in cluster
of glistening, orange-eyed, golden-yellow flowers, each about 2–2½ i
(5–6 cm) wide. It combines in a startlingly beautiful way with the ric
blue *Phacelia campanularia*.

Propagation *Seed is the only means of propagation. Sow thinly on site when th
weather warms up in spring. If it is inconvenient to sow seeds in the flowering site
sow clusters of three to four in small pots. Thin the seedlings to one to a pot prior to
planting out.*
Soil *A free-draining soil is essential; otherwise almost any soil is suitable, even a
very limy one.*
Position *A site in sunlight is essential. Hot, humid summer conditions are
not appreciated.*
Cultivation *Seedlings must be thinned with care, for damage to the roots of
those remaining can check growth.*

*When thinning the seedlings of
annuals, especially those sown too
thickly, it is possible to damage the roo
of those to be retained. To avoid this
press the fingers down on either side o
each seedling to be retained, to preven
root disturbance.*

Mirabilis jalapa

Mirabilis

One species in this genus is widely grown in warm countries and as a summer bedding plant in cooler ones. This is the Marvel-of-Peru or four-o'clock, *M. jalapa* from tropical America. It is always grown as an annual although it is a tuberous-rooted perennial, 2–3 ft (60–90 cm) or more in height with oval to lance-shaped, bright green leaves up to 6 in (15 cm) long. The stem tips bear a succession of funnel-shaped, 1 in (2.5 cm) wide, fragrant flowers in shades of red, pink, yellow and white, sometimes bicolored. Curiously, the flowers are petalless: what appears to be a funnel of fused petals is in fact a colored calyx. It combines well with other large summer annual or bedding plants, especially *Canna*, *Amaranthus caudatus*, *A. tricolor*, *Cleome*, *Dahlia*, *Helianthus*, *Helichrysum bracteatum* and *Ricinus*. Alternatively, single color selections can be planted with such summer bulbs as *Gladiolus* and *Galtonia candicans*. *Mirabilis* is also a good container plant and is ideal for sheltered patios.

Propagation *Cuttings can be taken from overwintered tubers in spring, or seeds sown earlier. Keep both at a warm temperature of about 65–70°F (18–21°C).*
Soil *Moist but reasonably well-drained, fertile soil is the ideal. Enrich poorer soils with organic matter.*
Position *A sunny site is best, though in warm summer areas some morning shade is tolerated.*
Cultivation *Young plants must not be set outside until fear of frost has passed. Water during dry spells. The plants must be lifted when frost damages the leaves, the tops cut away and the tubers stored in a frost-free place.*

Moluccella laev

Moluccella

Bells-of-Ireland is the charmingly unlikely name bestowed on *M laevis*, a native of the Middle East from Turkey to Syria. Shell flowe is an alternative vernacular name. Both refer to the large, bowl-shape calyces which persist long after the small, white, rather hidden flowe, have dropped. Depending on soil and situation, bells-of-Ireland ca grow 15–30 in (38–75 cm), in height, its erect stems clad in long stalked, boldly toothed, broadly oval leaves. In the upper leaf axil whorls of the 1 in (2.5 cm) wide green calyces appear and build up int compact spikes, which can be dried for winter arrangements. Th overall habit and bright green coloring of this plant make it a good fo for more brightly colored annuals, recommended examples bein species of *Clarkia*, *Nemesia*, *Petunia*, *Phlox drummondii* and *Verbena* hybrida. It also combines well with perennials and can be used to fi gaps between shrubs.

Propagation *Seed is the only means of increase. Except in areas with a long frost-free growing season, sow under cover in mid-spring at a warm temperature of about 60°F (16°C). Grow the young plants in 3–4 in (7.5–10 cm) pots prior to planting out.*
Soil *Well-drained and moderately fertile soil is required. Enrich poorer soils with organic matter.*
Position *A sunny site is best though a little shade is tolerated, especially in hot summer areas.*
Cultivation *Young plants must be watered during dry spells and kept free of weeds. If sown on site, the seedlings must be thinned with care.*

Myosotis sylvatica

Myosotis

The common or garden forget-me-not, *M. sylvatica*, is one of the best loved of all biennial flowers. Native to Europe and Asia and naturalized in parts of the United States, it is a tufted plant usually about 1 ft (30 cm) tall or a little more when in full bloom. In the first year, it forms compact tufts of oblong to lance-shaped hairy leaves. The following spring a sheaf of branched stems arise, bearing a profusion of sky-blue, yellow-eyed flowers. Several dwarf cultivars are obtainable, for example 'Blue Ball', of hybrid origin with the smaller perennial alpine forget-me-not, *M. alpestris*. There are also pink and white bloomed cultivars.

Propagation *Seed is the only means of propagation. Sow in nursery rows in early summer. If mature plants are left to seed, self-sown seedlings often appear.*
Soil *Moderately fertile, moist but not wet soil is the ideal, though reasonable results can be expected in poorer soils.*
Position *Although good flowering plants can be expected in sunny sites, a longer display will occur if grown in partial shade.*
Cultivation *Young plants should be grown-on in nursery rows, then transferred to their flowering sites in the fall. In very cold areas the protection of a cold frame may be necessary until the worst weather is over, when the plants can be planted out.*

In severe winter areas, forget-me-nots are not fully hardy and need protection. Either grow plants in pots that can be put into a greenhouse or lift from the open ground and place in boxes inside a cold frame for the winter.

Nemesia strumosa

Nemesia

The 50 species in this South African genus are allied to *Linaria* but have open-mouthed flowers which lack the long nectary spurs. Most widely grown is *N. strumosa 'Suttonii'*, a robust race developed by the English seed firm of Suttons. It grows about 1 ft (30 cm) in height and there is a dwarf strain about 7 in (18 cm) tall. Nemesia seeds are sold as color mixtures, embracing shades of red, pink, purple, blue, yellow and white. 'Blue Gem' is a forget-me-not cultivar and the only single color selection available. Individual flowers are about ¾ in (2 cm) wide.

Propagation *Seed is the only means of propagation. Sow in mid-spring and keep in a warm temperature of about 65–70°F (18–21°C).*
Soil *Well-drained soil of moderate fertility is ideal. Over-rich soil will promote soft, leafy plants at the expense of flowers.*
Position *A sunny site is required in cool summer areas. In hot summer areas, partial shade is advised. Nemesia does not thrive where the summers are usually hot and humid.*
Cultivation *Seedlings and young plants must be handled with care as even moderate root damage will check growth and can stimulate premature blooming. Young plants must not be set outside until all fear of frost has passed.*

If well grown, nemesia plants branch freely at the base, sending up a number of stems capped by flower trusses. Good plants are essential if a fine floral display is required.

Nemophila Menziesii

Nemophila

This North American genus of a dozen annual species contains two gems for a position at the front of a border. Most widely grown is *N. Menziesii*, still often listed under its older name of *N. insignis*. Perhaps even better known as baby blue-eyes, this is one of a mere handful of annuals with pure blue flowers, in this case sky-blue. Each bloom is bowl-shaped, about 1 in (2.5 cm) wide, the blue contrasted with a white center. *N. maculata*, the so-called five spot, is white with five purple spots. Both are spreading in habit but rarely attain more than 6 in (15 cm) in height.

Propagation *Seed is the only means of increase. Sow thinly on site in spring, just covering the seeds with soil, or in mild winter areas sow in the fall when larger, earlier blooming plants will result.*
Soil *A moist but well-drained and reasonably fertile medium is the ideal, though ordinary soil gives acceptable results.*
Position *In cool summer areas a sunny site is best, though some shade is tolerated. In warmer areas partial shade is best. Shelter from strong winds is advisable.*
Cultivation *Thin seedlings with care and keep free of weeds; the seedlings will require water in dry spells.*

Although lacking the clear blue of N. Menziesii, N. maculata *is equally attractive and even more striking with its sharply bicolored flowers of white and purple. Both species are native to California.*

Nicotiana alata

Nicotiana

This is the genus which contains the tobacco plant and gives its name to the deadly alkaloid, nicotine. It also contains the so-called flowering tobaccos, a worthy race of plants providing color and fragrance in the summer garden. The two species are the white, night-blooming *N. alata 'Grandiflora'* (*N. affinis*) and the red, day-blooming *N. forgetiana*. The latter is small-flowered and no longer grown, but its hybrid progeny with *N. alata* has given us the pink- and red-shaded cultivars, now so popular. It has also provided the day-blooming characteristic in several strains, for example 'Tinkerbell' and 'Nicki'.

Propagation *Seed is the only means of propagation. Sow under cover from early through mid-spring at a warm temperature of about 60–65°F (16–18°C).*
Soil *Moisture-retaining but well-drained soil of moderate fertility is the ideal. Enrich poorer soils with organic matter.*
Position *A sunny site is best but partial shade is tolerated, particularly in hot summer areas.*
Cultivation *Young plants must not be set outside until fear of frost has passed and the weather has warmed up. They must be watered during dry spells and kept thoroughly weeded.*

Flowering tobacco plants start off as minute seedlings that rapidly build up into tufts of oval leaves, which may reach 1 ft (30 cm) in length. Each tuft soon elongates and a branched stem arises, bearing a long succession of flowers.

Nigella damascena

Nigella

Although several species in this genus are cultivated, only one is popular and readily available from seedsmen. This is *N.damascena*, known as love-in-a-mist or sometimes as devil-in-a-bush. It is a slender plant to 1½ ft (45 cm) or more, with leaves divided into a mist of thread-like segments. The flower has five, pale blue petals surrounded by the same number of bracts cut into segments like the leaves. Modern cultivars have semi-double flowers that also come in shades of blue, purple, red, pink and white. The inflated horned seed pods look well in dried flower arrangements.

Propagation *Seed is the only means of increase. Sow on site in spring, or in mild winter areas in the fall.*

Soil *Ordinary, well-drained soil is suitable. Over-rich soil produces lush, leafy plants at the expense of flowers and makes them more liable to wind damage.*

Position *In cool summer areas a sunny site is best, though even here morning or afternoon shade is tolerated. In warmer areas partial shade is recommended, though they will not thrive in hot humid summers.*

Cultivation *Seedlings must be thinned with care and the young plants kept weeded; water in dry spells.*

The commonly cultivated species N. damascena *produces unique, inflated seed pods which can be used in dried flower arrangements. As soon as the pods start to turn pale brown, cut the stems and hang up in a warm airy place until thoroughly dry.*

Papaver rhoeas

Papaver

At least 50 different species of poppy are included in this widespread genus, three of which come within the scope of this book. *P. somniferum*, the opium poppy, is the largest flowered, with handsome gray leaves, but in the United States its cultivation is banned. *P. rhoeas* is the common or cornfield poppy of Europe and Asia. Normally deep scarlet, it has sported pink and white forms, some with picotee edgings, collectively called Shirley poppies after a famous English garden. *P. nudicaule*, Iceland poppy, is a perennial grown as a biennial, with red, yellow, orange and white fragrant flowers and deeply lobed leaves.

Propagation *Seed is the only means and must be sown very thinly and shallowly on site in spring, or in the fall in mild-winter areas.*
Soil *Ordinary, well-drained soil is suitable and reasonable results can be expected on quite poor land.*
Position *A sunny site is ideal but some morning or afternoon sun is tolerated.*
Cultivation *The seedlings are tiny and must be thinned carefully so as not to damage the roots of those that remain. They must be kept regularly weeded. As the blooms fade, remove them to promote further buds and maintain the display.*

The barrel-shaped seed pods of poppies have been likened to pepper pots. When ripe, a ring of small holes opens just under the lid of each 'pot'. Then, during spells of gusty wind when the plants swing to and fro, the tiny seeds are flung out. Ripe poppy seed heads can also be collected and used in dried flower arrangements.

Perilla frutescens

Perilla

One of the very few annuals grown solely for its foliage is *Perilla*. *P. frutescens* and its minor variants are the ones available from seedsmen. Roughly 2 ft (60 cm) in height, *P. frutescens* 'Atropurpurea' is a bushy plant densely clad with oval, boldly veined, dark purple leaves. *P.f.* 'Crispa', sometimes listed as *P. nankinensis*, has bronze-purple leaves with deep toothing and a crumpled appearance. All bear spikes of tiny, tubular, two-lipped white flowers which are best pinched out when young.

Propagation *Seed is the only means of increase, ideally sown under cover from early through mid-spring in a warm temperature of about 65°F (18°C). The seedlings are best pricked off into 3–4 in (7.5–10 cm) pots.*
Soil *Ordinary soil that does not get too dry is suitable, but if big, bushy plants are required a richer soil must be provided.*
Position *Sunny sites are best though partial shade is tolerated, especially in hot summer areas.*
Cultivation *Young plants should not be set outside until all fear of frost has passed and the weather has warmed up. Water them during dry spells.*

All the perillas mentioned above are foliage plants grown for their bold, colored leaves. The spikes of insignificant flowers tend to spoil the effect, so pinch these out as soon as they appear. Young flower spikes look like stem tips bearing crowded scale-like leaves instead of the normal foliage.

Petunia × *hybrida*

Petunia

None of the 40 species in this genus is now cultivated but the hybrid race derived from two of them ranks very high amongst desirable annuals. *P.* × *hybrida*, as this race is known, is highly variable. Among the dozens of cultivars are those of wide spreading and compact forms, more or less erect habits, some large and others small. The flowers, which in the single form are widely funnel-shaped, may be various shades of red, pink, purple, yellow and white, or may be strikingly bicolored. Double-flowered cultivars are available, as well as those with frilled or heavily crested petal edges.

Propagation *Seed is the primary means of increase. Sow in mid-spring at a warm temperature of about 60–70°F (16–21°C). The seed is very fine and is best mixed with several volumes of dry sand to aid even dispersal.*
Double-flowered cultivars can also be raised from cuttings taken in spring from overwintered plants.
Soil *Any moderately fertile soil is suitable, but it is advisable to enrich poorer land with organic matter.*
Position *A sunny site is best but some morning or afternoon shade is tolerated.*
Cultivation *Plants must not be set outside until all fear of frost has passed.*

Among the many petunia sports (mutations) are those with frilled or crested edges to the petals (far left). These can be single or double. Doubling of the normal smooth-petalled kinds also occurs. A fully double bloom is shown left.

Phacelia campanularia

Phacelia

O nly two of the 200 species of annuals and perennials in this genus are widely grown. Best known is the California bluebell, *P. campanularia*, a somewhat spreading plant to 10 in (25 cm) tall. It has oval, boldly toothed leaves of a somewhat grayish hue, and gentian bluebell flowers about ¾ in (2 cm) long. Very different is *P. tanacetifolia*, which starts off with a rosette of dissected, fern-like leaves, then elongates to 2 ft (60 cm) or so with a branching stem bearing numerous short spikes of small lavender-blue flowers. It looks charming with pink *Helipterum* or *Limonium suworowii*.

Propagation *Seed is the only means of increase and should be sown on site in spring. In mild winter areas, sow in fall and, if necessary, protect with a cloche.*
Soil *Ordinary, reasonably fertile garden soil is suitable. Too rich a rooting medium will encourage sappy, leafy growth at the expense of flowers.*
Position *A sunny site is best though some shade is tolerated, especially in the warmer areas. Hot humid weather is not appreciated.*
Cultivation *Seedlings should be thinned with care and regularly weeded.*

In areas with mild winters seeds of P. campanularia *and* P. tanacetifolia *can be sown in early fall. The young plants grow rapidly but, except in very mild areas, the young plants will need protection from cold winds and should be covered with cloches as winter comes. These can be a tunnel of plastic sheeting or of more traditional design in glass.*

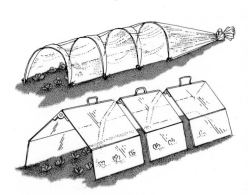

Phlox Drummondii

Phlox

For most gardeners this generic name means highly desirable perennial plants for flower beds, borders and rock gardens. However, there is also an outstanding annual, native to Texas, which has given rise to several distinctive color strains indispensable in the annual garden. This is *P. Drummondii*, a 1 ft (30 cm) species with pale green, oval leaves to 3 in (7.5 cm) long and a profusion of typically phlox-shaped flowers in a wide color range. Dwarf cultivars are available and also the highly distinctive *P. cuspidata* or Star race, with each of the five purple petals narrowing to a slender point.

Propagation *Seed is the only means of propagation. Sow on site when the weather warms in spring, or in areas with cool summers sow under cover in mid-spring in a warm temperature of about 60–65°F (16–18°C).*
Soil *Ordinary, well-drained but not dry soil is best. Too moist and rich a medium will promote soft leafy plants at the expense of flowers.*
Position *A sunny site is necessary for this annual, though a little morning or afternoon shade is tolerated.*
Cultivation *Young plants from a direct sowing must be thinned with care and kept weeded; water them during dry spells.*

The Star or Cuspidata race of annual phlox is the result of a highly distinctive sport (mutation) involving the petals. In the normal P. Drummondii, the petals are broadly rounded, but in the Cuspidata type, each petal tip is three-lobed, the center one drawn out into a slender point, giving a star-shaped outline to this attractive flower.

Portulaca grandiflora

Portulaca

Almost 200 species are listed for this genus but only one is grown for its ornamental appearance, *P. grandiflora*, which is sometimes called rose moss or sun plant. Both these vernacular names are apt as the flowers only open in the sun and the five-petalled flowers are not unlike small, wild roses arising from a soft cushion. The tiny narrow leaves are cylindrical and fleshy in texture but the effect *en masse* is somewhat moss-like. Semi- and double-flowered strains are most popular and come in a wide color range.

Propagation *Seed is the only means of increase. In warm sunny areas, sow on site when fear of frost has passed. Elsewhere, sow under cover in mid-spring in a warm temperature of about 60–65°F (16–18°C).*
Soil *Well-drained soil is essential and even dry sites are suitable, if not too poor.*
Position *A sunny site is essential because if the sun does not shine directly onto the buds they fail to open properly.*
Cultivation *Seedlings from seeds sown on site must be thinned carefully and weeded regularly.*

In sunny places, the rose moss or sun plant forms a dense mat of small fleshy leaves which become studded with glistening flowers that are available in a wide color range. It is a useful plant for dry banks or empty sunny nooks on a rock garden, making efficient ground-cover when well established.

Reseda odorat

Reseda

This genus contains one outstanding, fragrant annual, *R. odorat.* from North Africa. Commonly known as mignonette, it is an erec plant with bright green, curiously lobed leaves and spires of cream an orange blossom to 1 ft (30 cm) tall. The individual flowers are worth of close scrutiny, ideally with a hand lens. Each is composed of six whit petals, each of which is slashed into six narrow lobes. Within eac flower is a large bunch of stamens, tipped with orange anthers. Culti vated varieties, for example 'Crimson Fragrance' and 'Machet', gener ally have larger, more richly colored flowers.

Propagation *Seed is the only means of propagation. Sow on site in spring, or in mild-winter areas sow in the fall. Fall-sown plants will be bigger and flower earlier in the following year.*

Soil *A fertile, well-drained but not dry soil is the ideal. Over-rich soil will promote lush, leafy growth at the expense of flowers.*

Position *A sunny site is best, though in areas with hot summers some shade during the middle part of the day is desirable.*

Cultivation *Thin seedlings with care and keep weeded. Water in dry spells.*

*Given the soil and site to its liking, mignonette makes a bushy plant to at least 1 ft (30 cm) tall. Although quietly colored, it makes a useful foil for brightly colored annuals, at the same time scenting the air. It is particularly effective as an under-planting to Shirley poppies (*Papaver rhoeas).

Ricinus communis

Ricinus

The one species in this genus, *R. communis*, the castor-oil-plant, is a good example of a large shrub which can be grown as an annual. It is also known as castor bean and, in frost-free areas, can reach 15 ft (4.5 m) or more. Grown as an annual, it seldom exceeds 5 ft (1.5 m). Used as an accent plant among smaller growing annuals, it can look truly splendid with its big maple-like leaves 1–2 ft (30–60 cm) wide. Several cultivars with bronze, red or purple-flushed foliage are available, for example 'Gibsonii' which has metallic red leaves, and the new 'Impala' with bronze leaves. Castor-oil-plant is very amenable to pot culture and makes a fine specimen plant for a sheltered terrace or patio. It can also be used to fill a temporary gap in a shrub border.

Propagation *Seed is the main means of propagation. Sow under cover in early to mid-spring at a warm temperature of about 65–70°F (18–21°C). Sow the seeds singly in small pots; alternatively, in areas such as the southern States of the USA, where spring is warm and reliable, sow them where they are to grow.*
Soil *For big leaves and vigorous growth, plant in a fairly rich soil that is well-drained but not dry.*
Position *A site in full sun is needed in cool summer areas. In warmer places a little shade is tolerated.*
Cultivation *Young plants must not be set outside until fear of frost has passed and the weather starts to warm up. They should be watered in dry spells until well established.*

Rudbeckia hirt

Rudbeckia

Developed from *R. hirta*, the wild North American black-eye Susan, the gloriosa daisy is very much the product of modern plan breeding. The plant is larger and more robust than the wild plant reaching 3 ft (90 cm) or more with bigger, thicker-textured leaves while the flowers are almost twice those of black-eyed Susan, being 7 i (18 cm) as against 3–4 in (7.5–10 cm). The color range is also greater ranging from yellow to maroon, and there is a double-flowered race

Propagation *Seed is the only means of increase. Sow thinly on site in spring, or for earlier flowers and to provide young plants to follow spring bedding, sow in early spring under cover at a warm temperature of about 60–65°F (16–18°C).*
Soil *Ordinary, fertile, well-drained but not dry soil is the ideal. Within reason, the richer the soil the larger the flowers.*
Position *A sunny location is necessary for sturdy, free-flowering plants.*
Cultivation *Young plants must be kept free of weeds and watered during dry spells. Remove faded flower heads promptly to maintain the display.*

Black-eyed Susan in its wild state has yellow, daisy-like flowers with cone-like blackish centers. Through natural and artificially induced mutations (sports), various degrees of doubling have occurred. Best known is the 'Double Gloriosa', shown here, which looks like a florist's chrysanthemum with a small, dark brown eye.

Salpiglossis sinuata

Salpiglossis

This small South American genus contains one gem for the annual garden, *S. sinuata*, the so-called painted-tongue and an ugly name for so lovely a plant. It is allied to *Petunia* and the funnel-shaped flowers are similar but have five distinct lobes. They occur in shades of red, purple, blue and yellow, usually with a pattern of veining in one or two contrasting colors or shades. The plant is erect and slender to about 3 ft (90 cm). Dwarf cultivars also exist, including 'Splash', which reaches only 1½ ft (45 cm), and 'Bolero' which can reach 2 ft (60 cm).

Propagation *Seed is the only means of propagation. In warmer areas this can be sown thinly on site; elsewhere it is best sown under cover in mid-spring at a warm temperature of about 60°F (16°C).*

Soil *A well-drained but moderately moist soil, rich in organic matter, produces the best plants, though poorer soils still give fairly satisfactory results.*

Position *A sunny site is needed in cool summer areas, but where the weather is hotter some shade in the middle part of the day is necessary.*

Cultivation *Young plants should not be set outside until fear of frost has passed. They should be watered in dry spells until established.*

Seedlings of S. sinuata *are very small, but soon develop into tufts of elliptic, lobed or waved, sticky, downy leaves that are not without attraction. From among these leaves rise the erect, usually branched flowering stems. The tall-growing cultivars make good back-of-the-border plants or a distinctive centerpiece in a small bed.*

Salvia splendens

Salvia

Among the 700 species in this world-wide genus are the culinary herb, sage, and a number of very garden-worthy, ornamental, hardy perennials and shrubs, almost always grown as annuals. All the species have spikes of tubular, quaintly two-lipped flowers and in some cases the leafy bracts around them are also colored. Less visually startling than the over-familiar fiery red scarlet sage (*S. splendens*) is the mealycup-sage (*S. farinacea*), with long spires of violet-blue flowers in woolly calyces on stems to 2 ft (60 cm) or so. Highly distinctive is *S. Horminum* (*S. viridis*), with tufts of large, showy, purple, pink or white bracts at the tip of each 1½ ft (45 cm) flower stem.

Propagation *Seed is the usual means of increase. Sow seeds of the almost hardy* S. farinacea *and* S. Horminum *on site in spring, and those of the more tender* S. splendens *under cover in mid-spring at a warm temperature of about* 60–65°F (16–18°C). *If an earlier display of the hardy types is required, treat them in the same way as* S. splendens.

Soil *Fertile, well-drained but not dry soil is needed. Enrich poorer soils with organic matter.*

Position *A sunny site is needed in cool summer areas. In warmer places some shade is tolerated.*

Cultivation *Seedlings from an on site sowing must be thinned with care, watered during dry spells and kept weeded.*

Most species of Salvia *rely upon their flowers to attract pollinating insects. A few species, for example scarlet sage, have colored bracts (modified leaves) surrounding the flowers, to intensify the display of color. In* S. Horminum *(right) the small white flowers are insignificant, the role of attraction being taken over by a tuft of colored bracts at the tip of each stem.*

Scabiosa atropurpurea

Scabiosa

Comparatively few of the 100 species in this genus are cultivated but those that are make very worthwhile plants. Only one annual is regularly available, the sweet scabious, *S. atropurpurea*, native of southern Europe to Turkey. Also known as mourning-bride and pincushion, it is a slim, elegant plant to about 2 ft (60 cm) tall with fiddle-shaped basal leaves and smaller, deeply lobed upper ones. The 1½–2 in (3–5 cm) wide flower heads are basically red-purple, but all modern seed strains come in a range of colors from deep purple to red, pink, lavender and white.

Propagation *Seed is the only means of increase, sown on site when the weather warms in spring. In mild winter areas it can be sown in late summer or early fall or an earlier display.*

Soil *A fertile, well-drained but not dry soil is required for this annual but even dry soils are acceptable.*

Position *A sunny site is best but some morning or afternoon shade is tolerated.*

Cultivation *Young plants raised in warmth should not be set outside until the danger of frost has passed. Support plants with twiggy sticks in exposed places.*

Many of the taller, slimmer annuals are liable to damage in summer gales or rain storms. To prevent complete collapse, install some kind of support while the plants are small. Twiggy sticks are best for this task, giving overall support without looking unsightly. By the time the plants are in bloom, the sticks are generally obscured by the plant's growth.

Tagetes patula

Tagetes

Despite the curious, almost disagreeable scent of their foliage French and African marigolds are amongst the most popular annuals. In recent years there has even been something of a campaign to rename them American marigolds. French marigold, *T. patula*, and African marigold, *T. erecta*, are both natives of Mexico and central America. Most of the cultivars listed under these names are hybrids of the two. Much more elegant and with a greater profusion of smaller flowers and attractive, ferny foliage is the 1 ft (30 cm) tall *T. tenuifolia* 'Pumila' (*T. signata*).

Propagation *Seed is the only means of propagation. Sow under cover at a warm temperature of about 60–65°F (16–18°C) in mid-spring or later on site.*
Soil *Fertile, well-drained but not dry soil is the ideal. Over-rich soil will promote lush foliage at the expense of flowers.*
Position *A sunny site is best but some shade is tolerated.*
Cultivation *Young plants raised under cover must not be set outside until all fear of frost has passed. Thin plants raised on site with care and keep them watered in dry spells. Remove faded blooms regularly to maintain the display.*

Most of the popular cultivars of Tagetes *are double-flowered. As each flower fades, it becomes unsightly and for this reason alone it is worthwhile picking them off (dead-heading) regularly. Removal of faded flowers also prevents seeding and encourages the production of more buds.*

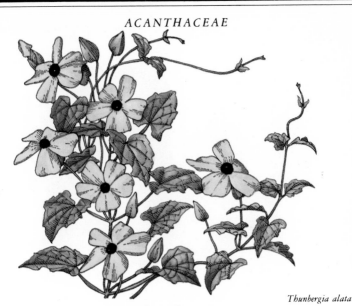

Thunbergia alata

Thunbergia

Several members of this large genus are important ornamentals in warm countries. Two of these, both climbing species, can be grown as annuals and are valuable garden plants because there are so few climbing annuals. Best known is black-eyed Susan vine, *T. alata*, a native of tropical Africa which can twine up to 10 ft (3 m) in one season. It has triangular, oval leaves on winged stalks and tubular 1½ in (4 cm) wide cream to orange-yellow flowers with chocolate-purple centers. *T. Gregorii* is similar but has bright orange flowers only and lacks the dark eye. Both species can be used to clothe a screening fence, provided the site is not too exposed and windy. A most effective way to use these plants is to let them ramble through a shrub which would otherwise be a rather dull clump of greenery.

Propagation *Seed is the usual means of increase. Sow singly or in pairs in small pots in a warm temperature of about 65–70°F (18–21°C).*
Soil *Fertile, well-drained but not dry soil is the ideal. Add organic matter to poor soil.*
Position *A sunny site is necessary, especially in cool summer areas. Where it is hotter, a little mid-day shade is beneficial but not essential.*
Cultivation *Young plants must not be set outside until all fear of frost has passed and the weather warms up. Support is needed for the twining stems, ideally twiggy sticks, string or netting.*

Tropaeolum majus

Tropaeolum

Some of the most useful and showy members of this genus are annual climbers and trailers. One of the most popular is *T. majus*, the so-called nasturtium. In its original form it can climb to 10 ft (3 m) or more, or trail along the ground, its round, shield-like leaves making good weed smother. Also popular are the bushy, non-trailing strains as typified by the Gleam Hybrids. Splendid for summer screening is *T. peregrinum (T. canariense)*, sometimes known as Canary-bird vine or Canary creeper. Its deeply lobed leaves are a perfect foil for the bright yellow, bird-like flowers.

Propagation *Seed is the primary means of increase. Sow on site in the spring when frosts cease, or sow earlier under cover, planting one seed in each small pot.*
Soil *Ordinary fertile soil is suitable, providing it is well-drained but not dry. Organic matter should be added to poor, sandy ground.*
Position *Sun or partial shade are acceptable. In hot areas,* T. peregrinum *appreciates some mid-day shade.*
Cultivation *Plants raised under cover should not be put outside until the possibility of frost has passed. Supports must be provided for climbers, preferably twiggy sticks, netting or a trellis.*

The common nasturtium can look most effective in a hanging basket. Fill a 10 in (25 cm) basket with potting mix and either sow two seeds in the middle or set one young plant. Remove the weaker of the two seedlings when they have two leaves. When the remaining seedling has four to five leaves, pinch out the growing tip, and when each of the branches that result have five to six leaves, pinch out their tips.

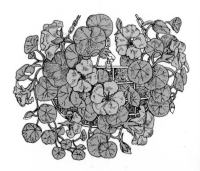

Verbena × hybrida

Verbena

Garden verbena, *V. × hybrida*, is a popular annual that has been grown for many generations. It arose as the result of crossing several South American species, around the middle of the last century. Really a perennial, it is a bushy, spreading plant with dark green, harsh-textured leaves and terminal heads of showy, almost phlox-like flowers in shades of red, purple, blue, pink or white. Very different is *V. rigida* (*V. venosa*), a wiry, erect plant 1–2 ft (30–60 cm) tall with many short, branching spikes of purple flowers. It combines well with pelargoniums and silver-leaved plants. Even taller (3–5 ft, 90–150 cm) is *V. bonariensis* from Brazil, Paraguay and Argentina. Also a perennial which can be grown as an annual, it has angular stems clad with pairs of rich green, oblong to lance-shaped leaves up to 4 in (10 cm) long. The small lavender-blue flowers are carried in head-like clusters from mid-summer well into the fall.

Propagation *Seed is the primary means of increase, and should be sown under cover in early to mid-spring at a warm temperature of about 60–65°F (16–18°C). Cuttings can be taken from overwintered plants in spring.*
Soil *Ordinary, reasonably fertile soil that is well-drained is the ideal. Over-rich earth will promote soft, leafy growth at the expense of flowers.*
Position *A sunny site is necessary for compact growth and free-flowering.*
Cultivation *Young plants must not be set outside until the possibility of frost has passed. They must be kept weeded and watered during dry spells until well established.*

Viola × Wittrockiana

Viola

Most of the 500 species of *Viola* are perennials for the rock garden and areas of shade. The garden pansy, *V. × Wittrockiana*, is a notable exception, always being grown as an annual. It is a hybrid between the small-flowered heartsease, *V. tricolor*, the mountain pansy, *V. lutea*, and the similar but larger flowered *V. altaica* from Turkey. Many strains and cultivars are available in a wide variety of colors and sizes, those thought of as typical pansies having a black mask-like blotch in the center.

Propagation *Seed is the usual means of propagation. For a winter and spring display, sow in a cold frame in late summer; for summer flowers, sow under cover in late winter or early spring.*

Soil *Ordinary garden soil is suitable. Dry conditions are not appreciated.*

Position *A partially shaded position is best for summer blooming pansies, more sun for the winter and spring flowerers. Hot summer areas are not tolerated.*

Cultivation *Young plants must be kept weeded and watered in dry spells. Dead heading will prolong the display.*

V. tricolor *(right, top) is the primary parent of the garden pansy (right) and the tufted pansy (far right). The latter arose as a cross between garden pansy and the long-flowering, tufted, horned violet,* V. cornuta. *Among the many tufted pansy cultivars are such famous old names as 'Maggie Mott' and new selections such as 'Funny Face'. They are fully perennial but are grown as annuals from cuttings and seeds.*

Xeranthemum annuum

Xeranthemum

The immortelle, *X. annuum*, can be described as Europe's answer to the Australian *Helipterum*. It is a less dainty and taller plant, 2 ft (60 cm) or so in height, but does not lack elegance. Its slim stems bear narrowly oblong leaves up to 2½ in (6 cm) long, each covered in dense white down on its underside, more sparsely so above. The daisy-like flower heads are composed of chaffy, petal-like bracts in shades of pink, lilac, purple or white. The plant combines well with ornamental grasses. They are excellent subjects for dried arrangements.

Propagation *Seed is the only means of increase. Sow on site in spring, or for an earlier display, sow under cover in early to mid-spring.*
Soil *A well-drained soil is essential; other than this any ordinary soil will do, even quite poor ones.*
Position *A sunny site is necessary, especially in cool-summer areas.*
Cultivation *Young plants raised under cover should not be put outside until the weather warms up. For drying, the stems must be cut as the top flowers open, tied in small bunches and then hung, flowers down, in an airy shed.*

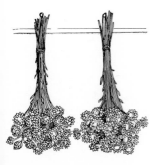

The way everlasting flowers are dried can greatly affect the finished product. Gather the flowers with as long a stem as possible the moment they are fully open. Tie in small bunches and hang head downward in an airy shed out of direct sunlight. Make sure the bunches hang vertically so that the stems dry straight; bent stems are difficult to arrange.

Zinnia elegans

Zinnia

Also known as youth-and-old-age, *Z. elegans* is especially popular in the United States, thriving in the long hot summers. Typically, it is an erect, sparingly branched plant to 3 ft (90 cm) with boldly veined, oval leaves in pairs and big double and semi-double flowers somewhat reminiscent of dahlias. Many cultivars and strains are available in a wide color range, some no more than 1 ft (30 cm) tall, others with quilled or waved ray florets. Small-flowered, bushy cultivars are largely derived from two other species, *Z. Haageana* and *Z. angustifolia*.

Propagation *Seed is the only means of increase. Sown from early to mid-spring at a warm temperature of 65–70°F (18–21°C) or on site when the weather has warmed up.*

Soil *A fertile, even moderately rich soil is ideal, providing it is moist but well drained.*

Position *A sunny site is essential, but sheltered, hot and humid corners are not appreciated.*

Cultivation *Plants raised under cover must not be set out until the likelihood of frost has passed and the soil has warmed up. Thinning of seedlings sown outside must be done with care. Water plants during dry spells.*

Zinnias are stiffly erect with opposite pairs of not especially noteworthy leaves. For this reason, they are best fronted or surrounded by smaller plants to mask the often bare stem bases and provide a foil for the flowers. Among plants suitable for this supporting role are species of Kochia, Perilla, Phlox and Verbena.

Glossary

Words in *italic* type denote other Glossary entries.

Annual A plant that grows from seed, flowers, produces seed and dies within the space of a single growing season. Compare *Biennial* and *Perennial*.

Biennial A plant that grows from seed, flowers, produces seed and dies within two growing seasons. Compare *Annual* and *Perennial*.

Coldframe Any type of unheated covered frame, admitting light and giving plants protection.

Cultivar Botanical term for a plant that has been developed through cultivation, as opposed to one occurring naturally in the wild.

Cutting Leaf, or portion of a leaf, or stem severed from a plant and used to produce a new plant.

Dead-heading The removal of dying flower heads to encourage further blooms.

Double Botanical term denoting a flower that has many more than the usual number of petals in its wild state. A semi-double flower has a few more than the usual number of petals, while the center of a fully double flower is filled with petals, possibly resulting in lack of stamens, rendering the plant sterile.

Drill Narrow furrow or groove made in the soil for sowing seeds in.

Dwarf A plant naturally smaller than those of the same species.

Floret A small individual flower which is part of the head of a composite flower (e.g. daisy). The central cushion-like disk floret is surrounded by ornamental ray florets.

Harden off The process of slowly acclimatizing plants propagated and grown in sheltered, warm conditions to the natural temperatures and conditions encountered when planted out.

Hardy Refers to plants that can survive outside throughout the year. Half-hardy plants will grow outside but will not withstand frost.

Hybrid A cross between two species, or varieties of species, indicated by the sign × in its name.

Humus The residue of organic matter that has decayed. Sometimes incorrectly applied to partially decayed matter, where traces of its original components can still be identified.

Mulch Organic matter, such as straw, grass cuttings or peat, applied as a top dressing around plants to provide additional nourishment. Mulch also suppresses weeds.

Mutation A plant that has undergone an accidental genetic change, leading to a new, inheritable feature. Sometimes called a sport.

Node The point on a stem where leaves and side-shoots develop, sometimes called a joint.

Nursery row (or **Nursery bed**) An area of the garden used for rearing plants before transplanting them to their permanent sites.

Perennial A plant that lives for at least three seasons, usually many more. Compare *Annual* and *Biennial*.

Pinch-out Removal of the growing tips of a plant to encourage side-shoots to develop.

Prick-out The operation of moving seedlings from where they have been raised to larger containers to allow room for growth.

Potting mix Specially prepared soil, usually of peat, loam and sand with added fertilizers, for growing plants in containers.

Rosette Refers botanically to the arrangement of petals and leaves in a rose-like pattern.

Stamen A flower's male organ, which carries and releases pollen.

Tendril The leaf or shoot used by a climbing plant to attach itself to the support it is climbing up.

Index

Acknowledgments
Dorling Kindersley would like to thank Simon Adams and Alison Chappel for their
special assistance and the following artists for the illustrations: David Ashby,
Will Giles, Vicky Goaman, Vana Haggerty, Nicki Kemball, Vanessa Luff,
Peter Morter, Donald Myall, Sandra Pond and Rodney Shackell.

Typesetting
D. P. Media, Hitchin, U.K.

Reproduction
Repro Llovet, Barcelona, Spain.